The
BUSINESS
OF
KOREAN CULTURE

The

BUSINESS

OF

KOREAN CULTURE

Richard Saccone

www.hollym.com

HOLLYM

www.hollym.com

First published in 1994
Third printing, 1996
by Hollym International Corp.
18 Donald Place, Elizabeth, New Jersey 07208, U.S.A.
Tel: (908) 353-1655 Fax: (908) 353-0255

Published simultaneously in Korea
by Hollym Corporation; Publishers
14-5 Kwanchol-dong, Chongno-gu, Seoul 110-111, Korea
Tel: (02) 735-7554 Fax: (02) 730-8192

Hardcover ISBN: 1-56591-033-8
Softcover ISBN: 1-56591-034-6
Library of Congress Catalog Card Number: 94-77532

Printed in Korea

INTRODUCTION

Everyday, talented businessmen lose money, time, and miss valuable business opportunities because they can't work effectively with their Korean counterparts. The frustration that develops, and the money often lost, is too frequently the result of cultural ineffectiveness. Whether Westerners are on their first trip to Korea or they've visited here for years, chances are they've found working in this wonderful country, at times, as puzzling as it is intriguing. Many Westerners spend years in Korea and still shake their heads at the different, often opposite, way things are done in Korea. The modern international business environment demands increased cultural awareness.

The Business of Korean Culture is intended to provide a general background of Korea, and answers to many of those questions, that may have stirred inside foreigners, about working and living in this exciting country. Each chapter supplies necessary information, in measured detail, concerning a variety of topics that a foreign business person should be acquainted with. Ultimately this knowledge should better prepare foreign businessmen for more efficient and successful use of their valuable time and effort while in Korea.

The information should be taken in the context of the entire text. Many of the chapters provide necessary links to the others. For example, becoming familiar with a little of the geography will certainly help understand how some of Korea's history was shaped. A firm grasp of both geography and history should facilitate understanding the origins and development of many cultural aspects of Korea. Armed with this foundation foreigners should be more able to apply some of the information and suggestions offered in subsequent chapters to their particular business situations.

The first chapter discusses some key concepts of Korean culture that are in many ways quite different from Western concepts. Every businessman, teacher, journalist or government official needs to be aware of and sensitive to these differences to work effectively in this environment. In comparing cultural contrasts, however, remember that the word Western is used rather loosely as I wrote this book from an American cultural point of view. I recognize that all Western customs are not the same, in fact, some German cultural norms for example, are very similar to Korean norms. There is often enough similarity in Western customs, however, to help other Westerners draw similar parallels.

Most of the chapter topics were selected from information I gathered, over the years, concerning difficulties foreigners related to me about life in Korea. My experience has been that many foreigners, whether businessmen, tourists, or government officials, register very similar complaints, usually based on common misunderstandings. All of the chapters are designed to provide information about specific aspects of Korea that will make living and working here somewhat easier and more understandable through identifying and explaining key concepts that are either different or often misunderstood.

No doubt readers will disagree about some of the generalizations discussed, but that comes with the territory. Cultures are complex by nature and descriptions rarely accurately explain every circumstance. Generalizations are intended to render complex concepts simpler, and more predictable, so take them in that context. Try to understand the text in a macro sense and apply it to individual situations accordingly.

Recognize that as a foreigner in Korea, there is some advantage to observing the indigenous culture. As Edwin T. Hall said so well in *The Silent Language*, "culture hides much more than it reveals and strangely enough what it hides, it hides most effectively from its own participants. "Ask an American to explain his own culture and chances are he will fail miserably. Similarly, ask a Korean and you're likely to discover the same result. A foreigner studying a different culture has the advantage of comparison, which can be a powerful tool in examination.

ACKNOWLEDGEMENT

In writing a guide such as this, as in writing almost any other book or article, the task can rarely be accomplished alone. Traveling around this beautiful country I have met countless kind and generous Korean people who have assisted me either by guiding me through their facilities, providing information, or by just offering sound advice. Without the help of such people, the difficulty of my task would have increased enormously. I know that as you travel around Korea, you too will meet some wonderful hosts who will make your experience that much more enjoyable.

In addition, I must thank my family who have always supported me in whatever effort I undertook. I do not deserve the wonderful wife and sons which have blessed my life.

Finally, but most importantly, I thank God Almighty who strengthened me every day of my life and allowed me to complete such a task. Without his help this book would not exist and whatever credit or glory is ultimately derived from it belongs to Him alone.

TABLE OF CONTENTS

1

BASIC FACTS

THE LAND

As one can quickly see by looking at a map, Korea is a peninsula in Northeast Asia which includes both the Democratic People's Republic of Korea (North Korea) and the Republic of Korea (South Korea). North Korea shares its northern border with both China and Russia. The Sea of Japan (Koreans call it the East Sea) lies between Japan and Korea's east coast. To the west, the Yellow Sea provides an important maritime link to China. The entire peninsula contains roughly 291,020 square kilometers making it approximately twice the size of Bulgaria or roughly the same size as the US state of Minnesota. South Korea makes up about less than half of the peninsula (98,486 square kilometers) and is close to the size of Hungary or Portugal or slightly smaller than the state of Ohio. South Korea is administratively divided into nine provinces and six special cities. The provinces are; Kyonggido in the northwest and surrounding the capital city of Seoul, Kangwondo in the northeast, North and South Chungchongdo in the west central region, North and South Kyongsangdo in the southeast, North and South Chollado in the southwest and finally Chejudo, Korea's largest island, less than 100 kilometers off the south coast (note: *do* means province in Korean).

Kangwondo is the largest province, at almost 17,000 square kilometers, and Chejudo is the smallest at just over 1,800 square kilometers. The special cities are large metropolitan areas, that by virtue of their huge populations, are administered separately. These include Seoul, Pusan, Taegu, Inchon, Kwangju and Taejon.

Many Westerners don't realize that Korea is a mountainous country, rugged mountains dominate the entire peninsula comprising 70~80% of the land area. Considering only about 1/5 of the land is arable, Korea is one of the most densely populated countries in the world at 438 persons per square kilometer, compared with India (252) and Japan(327). Within South Korea, the Taebaek mountains are a major mountain chain that run south following the east coast. The Sobaek mountains split off from the Taebaek and run through the southwest. The three highest peaks on the peninsula are in North Korea, the highest of which, Paekdusan, rises to 2,744 meters. In South Korea, the highest include Hallasan on Cheju Island, at 1,950 meters, Chirisan, 1,915 meters and Soraksan, 1,708 meters.

The Korean peninsula has a long coastline (about 17,300 kilometers). The coast of South Korea differs greatly from one area to the next. The east coast is known for its smooth shoreline and soft sandy beaches. Many beach resorts such as Kyongpodae Beach near Kangnung, and Haeundae Beach in Pusan, are popular summer attractions for vacationers. The relatively straight coastline, however, becomes progressively more irregular as it moves south and west. The south shore has an abundance of small islands nearby. Some 2,000 islands dot the south coast, many of them sparsely populated or even uninhabited. Turning to the west, the coast becomes increasingly more rugged with a highly irregular and rocky shore, hidden coves and large tidal differences. Inchon, on the west coast near Seoul, has some of the largest tidal differences in the world, reaching over 9 meters (about 30 feet). During low tide, huge mud flats stretching far out to sea, affect vital shipping in the area.

The many mountains of Korea help spawn scores of

rushing streams and rivers many of which have historic or geographic significance. Most of the major rivers flow west into the Yellow Sea. The Yalu River is by far the longest at 790 km. It helps form the border between North Korea and China. The Naktong, 525 km, flows south through the Kyongsang Provinces, while the Han River, 514 km, flows west through the capital of South Korea, actually splitting the city in half on its way to the Yellow Sea. The Taedong River, 439 km, flows through Pyongyang, the capital of North Korea. The eighth longest river, the Imjin, is only 254 km long but is geographically significant as it provides part of the current border between North and South Korea.

CLIMATE

Four distinct seasons offer a wonderful year-round variety of nature. Summers are fairly hot and humid with July through September susceptible to monsoon rains. July is usually by far the wettest month followed by August which is usually the hottest.

Winters are cold and dry with the lowest temperatures in January and February. Spring and Autumn seem short but both are very beautiful. Autumn is mostly free from the severe heat and pesky rains which makes it the most preferred time for festivals.

Most major international events, such as the 88 Olympics and the 93 Taejon Expo etc., were scheduled during this time for that reason. Autumn is also rich in beauty when the millions of leaves turn colors, and a trip to the mountains to view this magnificent spectacle is common for Koreans.

MAJOR CITIES

SEOUL - The capital of South Korea, is by far the largest city with over 11 million residents. It has been the capital of Korea since the beginning of the Yi Dynasty and celebrated its 600th anniversary in 1994. Seoul is much more than just a large city or even a capital to Koreans, it is the focus of most everything of importance. Education, government, business, culture, almost any aspect of Korean life has long been centered in this city. To live, work or have some connection to Seoul affords an important corresponding status business persons should not overlook.

PUSAN - Korea's second city is its largest port. Located on the southeast coast, it has long been heavily involved in foreign trade and has grown to a metropolis of over 4 1/2 million people.

TAEGU - Situated in the southeast in North Kyongsang Province, this vital city is close to many other important cities such as Pusan, culturally significant Kyongju, and industrial Pohang and Ulsan.

INCHON - Just west of Seoul, the city is Korea's second largest port. It is connected to the capital by major rail and highways.

KWANGJU - Located in the southwest province of South Cholla, Kwangju is vital to the economic and political life of that area.

TAEJON - A growing thriving city in the center of Korea, Taejon was the host to Expo 93, the most spectacular world's fair in many years. It has been expanding into a business and government hub, of sorts, in recent years.

POPULATION
Over 44 million people live in South Korea dwarfing the population of the North at about 22 million. By age, the largest group of persons are 15-19 (10.3%) followed closely by the 20-24 year old category (10.1%). According to 1990 statistics there are slightly more men than women in Korea. The single largest group of men are 20-24 year olds (10.5%), and the single largest group of women are from 15-19 (10.1%).

2

HISTORY

ANCIENT KOREA

Koreans have a long, proud history which can be traced back to about 2300 B.C. when the ancient kingdom of Choson was founded. According to legend it was formed by the mythical figure known as Tangun. Koreans still honor Tangun, and the foundation of Choson, with a national holiday in October. From the origination of Choson until about the first century B.C., the area, now known as Korea, was comprised of tribes and clans with no real political system as we know it. From about 76 B.C. however, three distinct kingdoms slowly formed on the peninsula. The Koguryo Kingdom to the north, spread wide on both sides of the Yalu River. It was famed for its effective cavalry and Koguryo warriors often battled Chinese and Korean neighbors over disputed territories. Paekche to the southwest, and founded about 18 B.C., at one time included present day Seoul. It was the first to adopt Buddhism as its national religion. Later, Paekche was said to have influenced the culture of Japan through Paekche art, culture and Buddhist thinking. Shilla to the southeast, was initially younger and weaker than the other two kingdoms. Although Shilla adopted Buddhism later than Paekche, many now famous Buddhist monks were produced from Shilla. Buddhism in the Shilla Kingdom appeared to be a uniting force that helped the kingdom prosper and grow stronger. The three kingdoms developed strong rivalries and were constantly at war with each other over territory and riches. They all had famous heroes, achievements and customs unique to their territory. All three kingdoms existed until 668 when the Shilla Kingdom finally overpowered the other two and united the peninsula under one ruler. The Shilla Kingdom quickly became the Shilla Dynasty and from 668 until 1910, Korea was united under three successive dynasties; Shilla (668~935), Koryo (935~1392), and Yi (1392~1910) (also known as the Choson Dynasty). It might be easy to remember the order by using the acronym "SKY" taken from the first letter of each dynasty's title. Subsequently, for almost twelve and one half centuries Korea was united, and steadily advanced socially, politically, and economically.

Once Shilla unified the peninsula, a single language and culture slowly developed. Kyongju was its ancient capital and much of the remains of that culture are preserved there and proudly displayed for all to see. With its absorption of both Buddhism and Confucianism from China, Shilla became quite literate in Chinese characters and its citizens took pride in advanced scholarly pursuits. Rebellions in outer territories weakened Shilla, in its later years, and it was eventually replaced by the Koryo Dynasty (from which Korea derived its name) in 935. Koryo lasted longer than Shilla and was initially famous for its cultural advancement. The world's first movable type was invented in Koryo, two centuries before Gutenberg invented it in the West. Also, fine ceramic pottery known as Celadon was invented during this period. During the later part of the Koryo Dynasty, the peninsula was invaded by the Mongols, who dominated the country from about 1231~1356.

Following the fall of the Mongols in China pressure began to build within Korea for a fresh beginning. After some years of struggle the Yi Dynasty was formed in 1392 and lasted more than half a millennium. During the Yi Dynasty (also known as the Choson Dynasty) Korea became even more Confucian. In the 15th century, the Korean alphabet was invented and many other scientific achievements were realized during the rein of one of Korea's most famous kings, Sejong. Late in the next century, the Japanese invaded (in 1592) and Korea suffered through an eight-year war. It was during this war that one of their famous naval heroes, Admiral Yi Sun-shin emerged to save Korea with the invention of his ironclad "turtle ship" and some brilliant naval maneuvers. In spite of eventually driving out the Japanese, Korea became an isolated country allowing little contact with the outside world other than China. As such Korea earned the name "Hermit Kingdom" and remained politically and socially isolated until the late 19th century.

FOREIGN RIVALRY OVER KOREA

By the mid eighteenth century a number of countries, including Japan, were once again trying to establish relations with the Hermit Kingdom. Russia, in need of warm water ports, had a keen interest in the tiny nation, while Japan, ever searching for more land and natural resources, also looked with a covetous eye at its western neighbor. China, Korea's "big brother", maintained the influence and strong relations it had developed over centuries. The struggle for control of the peninsula by these three powerful neighbors would eventually drive Korea to develop relations with another strong country, America. Although strong, America was geographically distant and much less of a threat to Korea's security. Korea hoped to use America to balance the growing rivalry among her neighbors. America, during this period, was itself expanding and in 1866, only a year after the American Civil War and a year before it purchased Alaska, America attempted contact with Korea. Its first attempts ended in disaster as Korea was not yet ready for relations with the West. In 1871, a skirmish between U.S. and Korean forces at Kangwha Island, west of Seoul, left hundreds of Korean soldiers dead and the chance for amicable relations souring. Through American perseverance and because of heightened threats from its close neighbors, Korea eventually signed the Treaty of Amity and Commerce with America in 1882, and America became the first Western nation to establish diplomatic relations with Korea. England, Germany and other European countries soon followed.

In the meantime, Japan was busy trying to wrestle political control of the peninsula from its neighbors. They first eliminated the strong influence of China after easily defeating them in the Sino-Japanese War of 1894~95. The victory provided them a much freer hand in Korea and a reason to station large military forces there. Next they moved against Russia, fighting the Russo-Japanese War of 1904~5, and defeating the Russians in a resounding naval victory. This left Japan in a very strong position to completely control Korea. Lastly, they cleverly eliminated the U.S. influence through negotiation. In 1905, the two countries signed an agreement which essentially concluded that the U.S. would recognize Japanese interests in Korea if Japan would recognize American interests in the Philippines. The stage was set for Japan to control the Korean peninsula, and in 1910 they annexed Korea. As a result, the Korean people ultimately suffered thirty five years under a brutal Japanese colonial rule.

KOREA UNDER JAPANESE RULE

Immediately upon annexation the Japanese took measures to completely control the peninsula. Key positions in industry and government were all occupied by Japanese, while Koreans were mostly relegated to low level employment. The natural resources of Korea were stripped to assist the economic advancement of Japan. The situation developed into a sometimes cruel occupation where Japan tried to forcibly absorb the country and its people into the Japanese mold. Koreans fought back by establishing a government-in-exile in Shanghai China, and initiating an Independence Movement within the country in 1919. The Japanese maintained their iron grip however, and in fact, tightened it. Japanese police tortured those who tried to resist and thousands of citizens were even sent to Japan for forced labor. By the late 1930's, Japan exerted strict control over various aspects of Korean life. They insisted Japanese be taught in schools and tried, in various ways, to extinguish Korean culture. Names of cities and towns were changed and citizens were forced to take Japanese names. Many older Koreans (who you may develop contact with) may speak Japanese because they learned it in school as a youth. A large number of Koreans still harbor, at least some, resentment of the Japanese because of the sometimes inhuman occupation.

LIBERATION, DIVISION, WAR

Toward the end of World War II, the defeat of Japan was fast approaching and the U.S. had no real plan for the fate of Korea. The Soviets entered the war in the Pacific late but were sweeping through Manchuria as Japanese resistance crumbled. The U.S. worried the Soviets could advance too quickly and occupy the entire Korean peninsula leaving no U.S. presence on the Asian mainland. A plan was quickly assembled for the U.S. to accept the surrender of the Japanese on the Korean peninsula. Planners observed the 38th parallel roughly split the country and encompassed Seoul, the traditional capital. They proposed the Soviets accept the Japanese surrender north of that line and the U.S. accept the surrender south of it. The Soviets agreed, but although the line was not intended to divide the peninsula politically, all did not go as planned and the division soon solidified.

Soon after the surrender, the U.S. proposed U.N.-sponsored elections but the North would not allow it.

They organized their own government and produced Kim Il-sung as president. In the South, U.N.-sponsored elections in 1948 produced Rhee Syng-man as South Korea's first president. The Soviets withdrew their troops from the North in 1948 and the U.S. withdrew from the South the following year, leaving only a military advisory group behind. The stage was set for a showdown between the two halves for control of their country. On 25 June, 1950, North Korea attacked South across the 38th parallel in mass, quickly overpowering the small, lightly armed forces in the south and in three days had captured the capital. They continued their push driving all forces down to what became known as the Pusan Perimeter. Actually the perimeter not only included the city of Pusan but an area from Pohang on the east coast to Masan on the south coast. Behind this line South Korean and American forces, quickly sent in to help, held the North Korean forces to a stalemate, buying time until more reinforcements could arrive. The U.N. Command had formed and General Douglas MacArthur became its first commander. Within a month he launched a daring counteroffensive comprised of an amphibious assault at Inchon, west of Seoul, with a simultaneous breakout of the reinforced forces from the Pusan perimeter. The offensive was a shocking success, catching the North Koreans by surprise and cutting off their supply lines. Seoul was recaptured and, in the following month, U.N. forces drove the North Korean troops all the way to the Yalu River on the northern border of Korea and China. In October, the Chinese entered the war in large numbers and drove the U.N. forces south allowing Seoul to be captured once again by the opposition. Seoul changed hands four times during the three-year conflict. A counteroffensive by U.N. forces recaptured Seoul and pushed the Chinese and North Korean forces back across the 38th parallel. Seesaw fighting continued until the Armistice on 23 July 1953. By the time of the Armistice, the line separating the two countries was no longer the 38th parallel but a much more jagged line which stretched across the peninsula north of the parallel in some areas and south of it in others. A Demilitarized Zone (DMZ) four kilometers across was established and has existed basically unchanged ever since.

MODERN POLITICAL AND ECONOMIC DEVELOPMENTS

After the war, President Rhee was elected several more times and South Korea began rebuilding their ravaged country with the help of the U.S. Thirty five years of foreign occupation and three years of devastating war destroyed the country. By 1960, economic failure and fraudulent election practices resulted in social disorder. President Rhee was ousted amidst huge student demonstrations. A weak interim government was elected and in 1961 General Park Chung-hee, took control in a bloodless coup. He was later elected president and served several terms until he was assassinated in 1979. During his administration many important economic and political developments occurred.

President Park Chung-hee Administration

Korea normalized relations with Japan and established diplomatic and economic relations in 1965. In that same year, South Korea deployed troops to Vietnam to assist the U.S. effort there. 300,000 troops rotated through Vietnam and almost 3,100 South Koreans were killed in that conflict. President Park began an economic program that changed South Korea from a country dependent on foreign aid to an expanding export-driven economy. Many of Korea's largest conglomerates (known as *chaebol*) began their rise to prominence during this period.

Political freedom was a persistent problem however and the president was not afraid to use martial law or other strict measures to maintain internal control.

In 1972, the Yushin Constitution was instituted which afforded the president much wider powers and authorized his use of emergency decrees. This caused even more domestic unrest and despite impressive economic gains, the absence of certain political liberties caused social and political turmoil. On 26 Oct. 79, President Park was assassinated by his CIA chief, Kim Chae-kyu, during dinner. Choi Kyu-ha became president but by 12 December another military general Chun Doo-hwan staged a violent coup to wrestle control of the military and then declared martial law.

The following year, nationwide demonstrations increased demanding the resignation of Chun, a new constitution, and an end to martial law. By 18 May 80, the situation had deteriorated and when key dissident figures were arrested, rebellion broke out in the southwest city of Kwangju. Dissidents seized the city driving out local police and military forces. Chun ordered in special forces that retook the city after bitter fighting and heavy casualties. Officially 191 citizens were killed but dissidents claim much higher tolls. By August, Chun resigned from the military and was elected president.

President Chun Doo-hwan Administration

President Chun tried to expand upon the economic progress enjoyed under President Park. In 1981, Korea was selected to host the Olympic games in 1988. Chun gambled that the construction and preparation for the games would help economic prosperity and unify the country politically. In 1986, Korea successfully hosted the Asian Games in Seoul as a prelude to the Olympics scheduled two years later. All appeared promising, but the legacy of the 1980 Kwangju Incident and absence of political freedom continued to haunt his administration. 1987 became a pivotal political year for South Korea. Widespread student demonstrations erupted early in the year and continued into the summer. By

June, the rallies were serious enough to threaten the stability of the country. In that same month, Roh Tae-woo, then leader of the incumbent political party, announced his support for sweeping reforms in the government, a new constitution, and presidential elections in December. His famous 29 June declaration all but halted the opposition. Korea prepared for the elections and the race was close. On November 29, just prior to the voting, Korean Airlines Flight 858, was blown up by North Korean Agents killing 105 passengers. The December elections proceeded and Roh Tae-woo was elected president. His mentor Chun Doo-hwan, stepped down marking the first peaceful transfer of power in seventeen years.

President Roh Tae-woo Administration

The 1988 Olympic games were held without a hitch. They were a great success and not only showcased Korea as an industrialized nation but opened the country to former communist nations which quickly initiated diplomatic relations. South Korea continued to advance toward the final step of democratization, electing a completely civilian president with no military background. A subsequent presidential election in 1992 produced Kim Young-sam as the new president. He was a perennial opposition leader whose time had finally come.

President Kim Young-sam Administration

The new president quickly began sweeping reforms that initially rocked the country. Fresh policies requiring asset disclosure of public officials revealed rampant corruption and resulted in numerous resignations and prosecutions. Further institution of true name banking rules deeply affected both the government and business culture. Rapid change occurred, to the displeasure of some, but President Kim maintained a high approval rating among the populace. Under his leadership Korea continued to grow as a modern democracy.

3

CULTURE

INDIVIDUAL VS. GROUP

The Orient in general, and Korea specifically, may accurately be labeled a group-centered society. Ideas and actions are considered in relation to how they are perceived by and benefit the larger group, as opposed to an individual. A Korean may belong to any number of groups such as family, company, business, school or a variety of others. These groups have a strong influence on their members and are an important part of an individual's life. They provide a vast support structure and a social network the tentacles of which spread wide across society. In Korean society, consensus is critical to promoting and maintaining harmony, the strength of the group, and Western style individualism is often viewed as selfishness. In essence, Koreans think group while Americans think individual. An example provided by Shin Mu-chol, a pubic relations manager for Korean Airlines, makes the point well. Shin said that while his group was traveling with a Western friend on a hot day, the Westerner noticed a little corner market and commented that he would like to stop to buy some ice cream. The Westerner emerged from the store with an ice cream bar only for himself. The group was disappointed. Shin explained to the man that even though it was such a small thing it was considered selfish of him not to bring ice cream for the rest of the group. The Westerner was surprised, as of course he was not a selfish person, but he was acting as an individual and not as a member of a group. This innocent example illustrates a fundamental difference in thinking some may not even realize. It is wise for Westerners to examine their actions and look for simple ways to fit in within the context of a group society.

Koreans take great pains to achieve and maintain group harmony, among subordinates, peers and superiors, at all costs. Consensus and harmony can play an especially significant role in decision making. Even high ranking officials must take time to build consensus on major decisions. Westerners tend to reach decisions quickly and sufficient authority may be vested in a single person, allowing that person to make a critical decision alone. A Korean manager is unlikely to have that luxury and in some cases may be forced to spend, at least some, time building consensus on a number of levels. Before pressuring a Korean client or colleague to make a decision be careful not to mistake the desire to build such consensus as stalling or indecision. Allow time for him to secure the proper support within the context of Korean culture. The consensus building process is often slower than Westerners may be accustomed to, but the results will likely be more favorable if the foreigner shows patience and flexibility.

Also consider that harmony and consensus-building may inhibit initiative and imagination. Westerners sometimes complain that a good number of their Korean employees and counterparts appear to lack initiative. Again consider that, in Korea, individual ideas or preferences are often subordinated to those of the group and subsequently individual ideas or preferences frequently do not surface. As a simple example try to notice how often Koreans, in a group, order the same item at a restaurant. They generally feel more comfortable conforming to group desires. It provides security and a sense of belonging. There are obvious advantages to group unity such as a strong support structure and a social safety net to name a few. Although it is frequently a difficult concept to accept for more self-reliant Westerners, remember it has served this culture well for centuries.

Another sharply contrasting aspect of the individual-group dichotomy is the approach to volunteerism. America, in particular, may be one of the strongest individual volunteer societies in the world. It is an integral part of American social obligation and volunteers are incorporated into uncounted service agencies throughout the country. Volunteering is respected and in some ways expected, especially for individuals of wealth and status. In a sense it is an individual's connection back to the group. Korea has many volunteers, make no mistake, but as a group-oriented culture Koreans need no connection to the group, it exists almost from birth. Instead, they often volunteer as groups, to which they already belong. Individuals volunteering for specific functions are much more rare. Volunteering as a group is more common. Foreigners are sometimes surprised and dismayed when their individual efforts at volunteering in Korea are not favorably received. Foreigners should not take it personally but understand the view of volunteering in the Korean context.

VERTICAL VS. HORIZONTAL SOCIETY

The West, prides itself on an egalitarian social philosophy permeating all aspects of society. America in particular, boasts a roughly horizontal social structure with a large middle class buffering the vast differences between rich and poor. Korea, conversely, is characterized by a more vertical social architecture with an established hierarchy and sincere loyalty to this more structured system. Of course, Koreans enjoy mobility up or down within the hierarchy, to a great extent, but whatever position they occupy carries a rigid, Confucian based, code of conduct which must be strictly observed. Individuals must show respect and use proper honorifics when speaking with those above them in the chain and may use less formal or even less respectful terms when speaking to persons lower in the hierarchy. An analogy can be drawn between this system and a typical military hierarchy where rank is a key determinant and manners and language are adjusted according to the positions of the individuals involved. In Korea, this type of vertical social system permeates society even reaching into the family. Specific terms describe each member of the family by position, such as oldest brother (*hyong*), younger brother (*dong saeng*), older sister (*onni*), younger sister etc. Age, position, education, family background and other distinguishing factors determine position in the hierarchy. Everyone, including foreigners, must recognize exactly where they fit and the relative position of others in order to properly interact. It is normal for Koreans to inquire about position and status at the first personal meeting, even before if possible, to ensure proper etiquette is followed. Learn to work within this system and take advantage of it by following the rules and not offending Koreans through ignorance of their ways. Foreign businessmen should make certain their position and title reflect the exact status they want to project, as it will generally determine how they are treated. When contacting others in business and government, Westerners should avoid the temptation to jump too many layers of the hierarchy, without the proper contacts and introductions, or their efforts may be quickly spoiled. Process and custom can be as important as substance. Foreigners who learn the rules early and use them to their benefit will reap the most success.

Another aspect of the vertical vs. horizontal contrast is the concept of fairness. For Westerners, especially Americans, an inclination to ensure fairness in all situations is important. Great effort is made in order to equalize situations to make them just. Americans often champion the underdog especially if the underdog has not been treated fairly. Koreans may view this concept differently. The best interest of the group and order of society may reduce the importance of individual fairness, or at least change how such fairness is viewed. Foreigners should remember that their concept of fairness is not universal, and while other cultures know fairness, it may be defined quite differently.

RELATIONSHIPS — THE KEY TO BUSINESS SUCCESS

Without a doubt, the individual network of relationships determines business success in Korea. Use care and patience in selecting and developing all relationships as they are vital to success. In establishing relationships know that Koreans are not "slap on the back" Americans. Be careful not to mistake politeness and hospitality for friendship. Koreans are gracious and friendly hosts, and their kind manner is often interpreted by Westerners as a sign of close friendship. This can be a costly miscalculation. Koreans develop friendships slowly over a long period. Eventually, relationships become extremely close and most often last a lifetime. It's natural for such relationships to be used for personal advantage. Personal and professional relationships are closely intertwined in Korea while normally separated among Westerners. In the West, true friendships are often formed based more on personal attractiveness rather than advantage. Westerners are reluctant to conduct business with friends, whereas Koreans are uncomfortable conducting business with persons other than friends: after all, they feel most people would not take advantage of a friend. Westerners are also often kind to persons they have no intention of developing a close friendship with which Koreans sometimes perceive as insincerity. In turn, Westerners sometimes perceive Koreans as cold because they may appear a little stand-offish to those they don't desire to develop relations with. Both perceptions arise from cultural misunderstanding. Koreans invest much time getting to know a potential business acquaintance as a person. They are generally more comfortable conducting long-term business with someone they know and trust, and Koreans fully understand how easy it is to be misled by first impressions. In general, they seek to probe past a person's official face and view the real person underneath. Smart Western businessmen want to do the same. However, Westerners often possess naturally open personalities and their first reaction to this may be "OK if they want to know the real me I'll open up, I've got nothing to hide." Be careful that sometimes the real self may be displeasing to others. The key is to be sincere and make others comfortable with your true personality without exposing too many negatives that might drive them away. This can be tricky and requires some forethought. Of course, one shouldn't deceive, but individuals may well want to protect certain aspects of their private life and background. Well what should a person do? A foreigner should portray himself as a reasonable, trustworthy, hardworking person, with some human frailties, but a person that is open-minded and sensitive to different cultures and points of view. Foreigners lacking these characteristics have some extra work to do. The key becomes how to properly convey positive personality traits to Korean business friends, and win their confidence and trust. Westerners should do so carefully, with much forethought, and release intimate personal information sparingly and incrementally. Koreans will form their overall impression from how foreigners act and speak, in a variety of situations, some social, some business, and smart Westerners are sensitive to this at all times.

Honesty is important in sincere relationships. Even if a Korean partner is not, he will expect it from a foreigner and respect him for it. Remember however, complete honesty can sometimes backfire. People in general, are comfortable knowing others have problems like them but can be frightened away by too much detail or too many problems. Knowing how to use honesty in the proper measured amounts can be critical to developing long-lasting relationships. Again a complete "warts and all" approach is not recommended, especially early in a relationship. Pointing out another's failings, no matter how well intended or kindly presented, is not recommended. Such honesty is best avoided unless asked for specifically and then should be given sparingly.

Another aspect of honesty involves admitting ignorance. Americans, in particular, respect a person who admits he does not know. Not knowing a particular piece of info is not a shame although it most often carries the obligation of finding out, after such an admission, if the person questioned is expected to possess the knowledge. For Koreans, however, acknowledging an inadequacy such as, not knowing, can mean a loss of face. As a result, Koreans may not admit they do not know and may attempt to answer even though they could be wrong. Foreigners too, may lose face in Korean eyes when they admit they do not know especially if it is reasonable to expect the foreigner to possess that particular knowledge. Foreigners should consider this during discussions with their Korean counterparts. When such a situation is encountered there are times it may be wiser to talk around the subject, or even suggest the issue is still under study, rather than abruptly admit ignorance.

Sometimes, Koreans rely on the integrity of a foreigner before that of other Koreans because they know the customs and values of the two cultures are quite different. Don't disappoint in this regard. Make certain to complete all agreements exactly as promised, even though the Korean partner may not. Honestly explain problems if they develop and Koreans will likely concede changes to maintain harmony. Be flexible enough to bend a little concerning their broken promises. If possible, don't insist on sticking too closely to a written contract. Koreans view a contract as a mere piece of paper much less important than a sincere relationship. Koreans more easily forgive broken contracts, caused by extenuating circumstances, than Westerners. Try to do the same. Knowing a foreign partner can sometimes abide by Korean customs may result in short-term losses but may ultimately translate into devoted long-term business.

The element that acts as a binding force in a Korean relationship is obligation. Basically, there are two kinds of obligation, reciprocal and social. Reciprocal obligation is performed to repay a favor or other specific act of benefit to the other person. It is a common and an expected outgrowth of friendship in Korea. Friends expect to use their relationship for personal advantage, and it is difficult to turn down a friend when so obliged. In some Western countries, America for example, such circumstances are generally avoided, especially by persons in authority. Americans believe certain obligations blur an individual's ability to maintain fairness and objectivity. There are even laws against such activities in public service. Americans may feel manipulated and offended if they believe their relationship is being used by a friend in order to obtain some favor or advantage. Americans prefer to receive favors with "no strings attached," and are more willing to repay of their own volition. It's one of the reasons Americans generally pay their own way; to avoid the potential obligation. Conversely, social obligations are those that require no repayment but often stimulate such action from the sincere wish to return kindness even without the obligation to do so. Such feelings often spring from shared experiences and sincere liking for another. For example, if a neighbor helps another carry heavy grocery bags into his home, the one neighbor may thank the other and forget about it. There is no need to wait for him to go shopping and return the favor. But because that act of kindness generated a good feeling, the one neighbor may decide to perform some other act of kindness for the helping neighbor, even though it is unnecessary and unsolicited. In this sense it is not an obligation at all but individuals are often drawn to return such kindness as if they were required to. With this type of obligation, however, there is no real pressure to repay if a person does not wish to. Circumstances of this type are generally more appealing to Americans in particular.

One way to strengthen an existing relationship, especially when dealing with an elder, is to ask their advice. I call it the mentor approach. The matter need not concern the specific business that person is engaged in and it may actually be more beneficial to seek advice about some completely unrelated subject. After choosing to consult a business friend in this way, try to make the approach during a special meeting or at a special private opportunity. Never ask for sincere advice off the cuff, for example, at a social mixer or reception etc. Schedule a specific appointment or take advantage of a situation offering some private time together to discuss such a matter. Be sincere and point out that the reason that person is specifically being consulted, is because his knowledge and experience in life, business, etc., are highly valued. It requires a little humility to ask another for advice and Koreans respect this virtue. If done properly the mentor will perceive the request for advice as a compliment. In turn, he will most likely be flattered and anxious to provide honest counsel. He may even provide further help by introducing others who might assist. Do not pose a trivial matter or fabricate a problem for this purpose as the mentor may see through such a ruse and could be offended or may insist on providing unwanted assistance. Instead take advantage of special opportunities to request advice, sometimes even if it's not needed. A foreigner sincerely confiding in a Korean older than himself, will foster a special feeling for the elder, help draw the two closer, and likely yield a perspective the foreigner had not thought of. Foreign businessmen must be careful however, not to choose serious personal problems that might portray them in an extremely bad light. This could actually do more harm to the relationship than good. In addition, don't attempt the mentor approach too early in a relationship or it may be ineffective. Wait until time and frequency of contact have allowed the seeds of friendship to take root. Then the mentor approach will act as a fertilizer to nourish the relationship and help it grow stronger more quickly.

When developing business relationships remember that hundreds of separate contacts are needed to make your network most effective. Of course no one can hope to develop close relations with all of them. A smart businessman divides contacts into prioritized layers and spends appropriate amounts of time with each. I recommend the following three layers fashioned much like a pyramid:

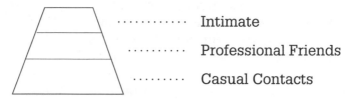

.... Intimate

.... Professional Friends

.... Casual Contacts

Intimate - Occupying the uppermost and smallest portion of the pyramid, this group is composed of the closest social and professional friends. Within this tight group it is common to know and even socialize with family members. Some obligations are traded between them and it is comfortable to ask their help or advice. Foreigners should spend regular and frequent time nurturing these relationships. Among close friends such as these it is not uncommon for Koreans to schedule monthly meetings or other regular get-togethers.

Professional Friends - This group shares mostly professional and some social activity together. Members of this group know each other well enough to trust in some business activities but are not involved in deep personal relations.

Casual Contacts - Visit often enough to remain on a friendly basis. These people can be relied on infrequently to provide help or assistance. They may not be close but because of a friendly relationship they can be expected to provide better service or assistance in time of need. This group may include persons from any position or level from top managers and bureaucrats, to secretaries and service personnel, etc.

Because there is not time or money enough to take care of all these people in the same manner, a good businessman spends an appropriate amount of time and money on individuals from each category to obtain the depth of relationship desired.

Grow Strategic Contacts - Any foreigner planning on building long-term business in Korea (it's a must for success) should seriously consider developing strategic contacts for their relationship network of the future. Begin early, spotting bright young people in related companies or technical fields, and invest some time and money establishing and nurturing relationships. Invest early and as these individuals ascend the corporate ladder they will become strategic allies, either assisting directly or facilitating valuable introductions to those who will.

NTERPERSONAL COMMUNICATION
— BRIDGING THE CULTURAL GAP

Korea is one of many countries labeled as a high context culture. This label was described extensively by Edward T. Hall in various scholarly studies. (Note: Edward Hall spent over fifty years researching and studying intercultural communication. He has several books on this subject including *Hidden Differences,The Silent*

Language, and *Beyond Culture*.) High context communication is characterized by physical, non-verbal communication without reliance on encoded verbal cues. Quite a few Western nations, especially including America, are relatively low context cultures relying much more on elaborate verbal communication. Even though the high context/low context dichotomy is not "either/or," but best viewed on a continuum, it is easy to see the contrast between East and West in the basic philosophy of interpersonal communication. In high context cultures, like Korea, the environment contains much of the message. Mood, expressions, the situation, even silence itself all provide large pieces to the communication puzzle. In low context cultures, like America, detailed and often repetitive explanations are critical to ensure accurate communication. As such, members of high context cultures, who by nature verbalize less, are sometimes viewed as mysterious, intriguing or even sneaky and untrustworthy, because their intentions are not often clearly expressed in words. Members of low context cultures are sometimes viewed as verbose, redundant and insincere. These mis-perceptions are sometimes amplified when such diverse cultures meet in situations requiring close working relations.

Because much of the message is in the context, Koreans rarely come directly to the point verbally. They expect others to decipher their meaning without such directness, which they consider somewhat offensive or uncultured. A simple but common example is the Korean letting the host know he left the door open. Rather than directly mentioning that the door is open, he might choose to note a slight chill in the air, which tactfully alerts the host that the door is open without embarrassing him. A better and more complicated example could be drawn from the typical married couple involved in a quarrel. The next day the spouse is moping around the house in bad spirits. A Western spouse would likely approach the other and ask the obvious, "what is wrong" and suggest discussing a resolution. The Korean spouse is more likely to discern the problem without speaking, and try to make amends by presenting a small gift or making a kind gesture without actually mentioning the quarrel. The difference in approach is significant. Koreans expect this type of sensitivity, especially among friends, and consider it a sign of culture, good manners, and proper upbringing.

If forced to verbalize, the indirect approach is again employed, talking around a difficult subject expecting the receiver to decipher the message long before it's necessary to come to the point. This can be tiring for foreigners, especially during fact-finding discussions or intense negotiations. Americans in particular, like to come to the point quickly and resolve issues directly. Koreans are generally not comfortable with this approach. Foreigners will do well to exercise patience during those discussions as impatience will be perceived as a negative and cause the foreigner undo frustration.

Another stark contrast between cultures involves the use of eye contact. In the West, especially in America, direct eye contact is expected during conversation. A person who can't maintain eye contact may be suspected as untrustworthy. There is a saying "look me in the eye and say that". Westerners feel that a person will somehow respond more honestly when peering into another's eyes. Eye contact may also show interest and attention and a lack thereof, in a conversation, can offend. In Korea, eye contact is much less prevalent. It is impolite to look into another's eyes. especially those of an elder, and so sometimes when Koreans are showing respect to an older Westerner, he may think the Korean is rudely showing disinterest. It is fairly easy to see how such contrasting fundamental elements of communication can be misunderstood between cultures.

The American penchant for exaggerating to make a

point is often confusing for high context Koreans. Sayings like, "it takes forever to catch a taxi in Seoul" or "I've been waiting ten years for the bus" are just simple examples of a concept that puzzles those who consider language as just a small part of necessary communication. Make no mistake, exaggeration is not unknown to Koreans but the degree and frequency of its use is not nearly as prevalent. In addition to exaggeration, Americans in particular, have a tendency to see issues as an "either/or" dilemma. For example, "either you're with me or you're not", "either you like it or you don't", "either we do it this way or we scrap the whole deal", etc. This position can be very frustrating especially when answers to complex situations cannot be distilled down to simplistic alternatives. Similar to the "either/or" dilemma, Westerners and Americans in particular, may tend to speak in absolutes. For example, "you're *always* late", "they *never* meet their suspense" etc. Again, absolutes can confuse or cause resentment, even though the foreigner may consider it merely a figure of speech. Foreigners should examine their own speech patterns and attempt to eliminate parts that may impede smooth communication.

UNDERSTANDING THE UNSPOKEN

Non-verbal cues form just a small portion of unspoken communication. But even non-verbal communication is widely different between East and West. Americans for example, are a virtual carnival of facial expression and hand gestures that Koreans often find amusing. The wink, that wonderfully simple and versatile method of communicating at least five different meanings, is not naturally part of Korean culture and the sight of it usually tickles Koreans and produces broad smiles. The rapid raising and lowering of the eyebrows, to show interest, is another non-verbal cue that can induce laughter from a surprised Korean onlooker. Tongue in cheek, rolling of the eyes, licking the lips, among others, are all foreign to this country. Still others, such as nodding the head up and down for yes and sideways to mean no, pushing out the bottom lip to show disappointment, pursing the lips to display anger, and an inquiring raise of the eyebrows are similar to both cultures.

Hand gestures may also provide some examples of cultural contrasts. The Korean gesture for money is demonstrated by connecting the thumb and index finger, to form a circle, with the other three fingers pointed downward. Americans signal money by quickly rubbing the thumb across the tips of the four fingers, palm up. The shrug of the shoulders, with the head tilted to one side to communicate "I don't know", has no equal in Korea. The index finger placed perpendicular to the lips, signifies, "Be silent", in both cultures but can also mean "Keep a secret" to Americans.

But the title of this section refers to a much deeper form of non-verbal communication involving recognizing and sharing emotions. Western culture knows it in the form of empathy that comes from long-term association with another like a close relative or spouse. Most married couples have probably experienced a situation where one spouse knows what the other will say before it is spoken. Or when one spouse can predict the other's reaction before a response actually occurs. With a little effort one spouse can probably feel as the other feels, in certain circumstances, even though the other never expresses that feeling verbally. That type of empathy, while reserved for more intimate relationships in the West, is much more common in casual interpersonal contact in Korea. The term describing the ability to discern and interpret these feelings non-verbally is "*nunchi.*" This skill becomes a powerful tool in ensuring harmony in interpersonal relations by effectively reading another's feelings. Once this skill is developed, a large portion of routine communication can transpire without a word or so much as a raised eyebrow. People can learn to feel each other's mood routinely. Communication requires participants to focus on non-verbal behavior that provides clues to inner feelings. Foreigners must use care, when listening and observing, not to screen out behavior they should be examining and interpreting. Westerners who rely on detailed and repetitive verbal communication to feel comfortable understanding another's mood, can be confused in Korea where much interpersonal communication is conducted non-verbally. Conversely, Koreans typically do not understand why Westerners insist on verbal communication in situations better conveyed non-verbally. For example, Koreans wonder why Westerners must continuously say "I love you" to make a partner sure of their intimate feelings. Koreans believe such emotion is more sincerely communicated non-verbally. Again, the example used in a previous section seems appropriate; if a spouse is moping around the house, Westerners would tend to question what is wrong and try to resolve it verbally. Koreans, on the other hand, might detect the bad feelings and try to cheer up the person with a gift of flowers or an act of kindness, without discussion. While understanding the unspoken is certainly a challenge, it's a skill that pays big dividends for foreigners who can develop and utilize it effectively while working in Korea.

KIBUN — WHAT MAKES KOREANS TICK?
To accurately describe this distinctly Oriental concept, in Western terms, is a difficult task. In short, *kibun* is the essence of the Korean spirit. More than a mood, and more than mere feelings, one might say it is a combination of self-esteem, mood, feelings, and a person's inner spirit. Recognizing its mere existence, however, is not quite as important as understanding its condition and well-being. Maintaining harmony of *kibun* is of great significance to Koreans. Harmony of spirit is the balance of life, the stabilizer of nature's opposites such as yin and yang, male and female, good and evil etc. Of course to disturb this delicate balance with additional negatives, especially if presented abruptly, destroys the *kibun*. As such, Koreans generally hesitate to introduce negatives directly, and are reluctant to present unpleasant news, or say "no" abruptly. They are also hesitant to relay bad news to elders, especially in the early morning, for fear of ruining that person's *kibun* for the entire day. Foreigners should consider these courtesies when dealing with Korean business friends, especially when discussing major issues of significant impact. A foreigner's approach and ability to smoothly relate negative information, can make a significant difference with how Koreans react, to the specific issue, and how they remember him long afterward. While negatively influencing one's *kibun* is unwise, positively influencing it is certainly welcome and encouraged. The foreign businessman who strives to pump his friends' *kibun*, making them happy even in times of difficulty, is on the road to close cooperation and success. The actual method of pumping one's *kibun* is considerably more complicated than mere flattery. It's a combination of making a person feel comfortable, relaxed, unthreatened and happy all at once. To successfully accomplish

this, avoid situations that may even slightly embarrass, be flexible enough to overlook slight mistakes, especially in English language, and keep a cheery spirit at all times. Allow them to discuss matters of their own interest and respond favorably throughout the conversation. This really isn't difficult as Koreans are great guests and hosts. However, little things foreigners sometimes do, often without realizing, can quickly spoil a pleasant mood. Take special care in wording negative comments or replies. For example, if asked "Do you enjoy kimchi" (Korea's national dish) instead of frowning and saying "Oh no, it's too hot for me" etc., consider responding, "Yes, it's delicious but I'm still developing a taste for spicy food." Koreans will understand the message without being offended. In fact, they generally take notice of and appreciate a foreigner with tact. Westerners are frequently more comfortable providing completely open and honest answers to questions while Koreans prefer a more indirect approach which considers the feelings of others. It might be argued that Americans generally provide more bluntly honest feedback expecting the other person to be "thick skinned" and capable of accepting the truth. Koreans tend to provide indirect feedback assuming the other person's skin is "thin" and trying to avoid inflicting any emotional pain on them. Foreigners who make the extra effort to respect Korean custom will be viewed as a very attractive partner in Korean eyes and someone they will rush to develop a relationship and conduct business with. Reading *kibun* is critical to fostering and maintaining the necessary harmony. The Western businessman who works to develop skills and sensitivities to other's *kibun* will be on the path to stronger and more productive relationships.

FACE — SAVING IT IS IMPORTANT

As *kibun* is a reflection of the inner spirit so face is the essence of one's outward image. This concept is found in both Western and Oriental cultures, in one form or another, and includes both individual, social and professional reputation. The concept of face is readily associated with Asian culture. However, although often disguised and not easily recognizable, face, in various forms, is certainly part of Western tradition also. Westerners sometimes try to spare another's feelings or protect a reputation by employing means such as "giving the person an out" or "throwing a bone" to someone who is about to lose out. Westerners may not readily recognize it as such, but in essence it's done to protect a person's outward image or "face." In the Orient, the emphasis and importance of this outward image, are magnified in comparison to the West. Maintaining or saving face is vital when dealing with Koreans in any type of social or business setting. Be sensitive to actions that might cause them to lose face. As such, attempt to avoid situations that could publicly embarrass or make them feel uncomfortable, when possible.

In negotiations, it's wise to compromise, at certain times, to allow a Korean partner to save face or maintain a respectable image. Allowing him to lose face could result in a tactical victory but possibly a devastating strategic loss. Koreans may spend well beyond their means to entertain, make an impression, or fulfill an obligation. Again, this is often done to save face. Pardon me if I dare quote a Japanese Emperor to illustrate how Koreans feel about this principal: "To lose face is everything, but to lose everything is not necessarily to lose face." Somewhat exaggerated but it makes a point.

Remember also that when presented with an embarrassing situation or one where a foolish mistake was made, Koreans often smile. The smile does not indicate a lack of regard for the mistake, it's their way of trying to smooth over the public embarrassment from it. This is sometimes confusing to Westerners, but face is largely responsible for this Korean reaction.

Recognizing the importance of face and dealing with it appropriately can save time and money, overcome resistance, and prevent unnecessary interpersonal difficulty.

PERSONAL SPACE — A DIFFERENT PERSPECTIVE

A very interesting concept quite different from the Western version, the Korean concept of space is sometimes the source of frustration and misunderstanding among foreigners. It may help to first examine the American concept for comparison with the Korean. In the 1960's, one researcher (Edward T. Hall, 1966) studied American personal space and discovered a four-tier system of interpersonal distances. The first, from about 0 to 1/2 feet, he labeled an intimate zone; from 1/2 to 4 feet, a personal zone, from 4 to 12 feet, a social zone and over 12 feet was labeled a public zone. While the distances may not be so exact, as a group, Americans are sensitive about the boundaries of these zones and become uncomfortable when others ignore them. For example, in America, if one person enters another's intimate zone, for conversation, the person may find the other retreating to add the proper distance. If someone brushes or bumps another, even in a crowded area, in effect they invaded that person's intimate space and American culture requires that a person acknowledge and apologize for such an act by begging pardon or saying "excuse me". Ironically, Americans are somewhat more territorial and often lay claim to space even temporarily. For example, anyone who has ever attended a class or briefing

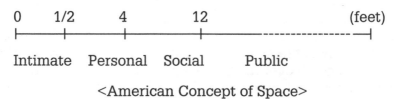

<American Concept of Space>

without assigned seating may have noticed that after a break, most people return to the same seat and become offended if someone takes that space from them even though other equal open spaces are available. Koreans, on the other hand, live in one of the most densely populated countries in the world and haven't had the luxury of large individual spaces. They frequently bump into each other on crowded streets, subways, buses and markets, and are forced to routinely share precious space with others. They normally don't apologize for straying too close to another, in these situations, because, by their culture, they have committed no violation. Often foreigners visit Korean markets or crowded streets and remark how rude or pushy Koreans are for jostling or bumping into them without apology. This may be a result of not understanding different notions of space.

The issue of touching, in general, is also different between East and West. Some foreigners may be surprised to see Korean members of the same sex, both male and female, holding hands or walking with their arms around another's shoulder, without any sexual connotation. This type of behavior is normal between close friends. Among men, foreigners may be surprised to find a Korean friend clasp his hand when meeting or place his hand on the foreigner's leg during a drinking party or friendly discussion. Again, this is not a sexual advance but a simple gesture among friends. This can be somewhat unnerving for a foreigner unaware of this behavior and may still be difficult to become comfortable with even after learning of it. Conversely, some American customs involving touch, like the slap on the back, or the gentle punch in the arm, are considered very rude by Koreans.

Office space provides a glimpse at another cultural contrast. As might be expected from an individual-centered culture, it is normal to expect individual offices in Western society. Even if offices are not completely walled they are often separated by partitions and individually decorated. It is common to see diplomas, family pictures, and others items displayed to personalize that particular space. Koreans are more likely to encourage open group offices with many desks aligned with a supervisor in a position to view the subordinates. Individual office spaces are more rare and reserved for high ranking positions in Korea, although recently some large businesses use partitioned space in a limited sense.

Foreigners tend to view Koreans through the spacial rules of their own culture instead of the rules of their hosts. Understanding the differences associated with this complex concept may help promote better understanding between the different cultures.

KOREAN TIME — SOMETHING TO PREPARE FOR

The patience of the Orient and good manners dictate that gentlemen are rarely in a hurry. Consequently Koreans may be five, ten, twenty minutes etc., late for appointments. Do not assume a Korean partner will not arrive because he is excessively late and when he arrives he may not apologize because, by his culture, he has committed no violations. The Korean will likely expect the foreigner to know that he came as fast as he could and expect the foreigner will not be offended. It helps to plan accordingly to preclude frustration and embarrassment. A foreigner can help himself by not scheduling appointments too closely. Planning a little extra time between meetings can ultimately relieve the pressure if a partner is late. It may also prevent any frustration, anger or disappointment, from being communicated, either verbally or non-verbally, which would definitely injure another's *kibun* and possibly damage a relationship. Of course, in a modern industrialized country like Korea, many businessmen have grown to understand and respect the need for punctuality. It still pays to remember, however, there are differences in the way the two cultures generally view time.

It is not uncommon for meetings, movies, and other public events to begin a little late. The Western style pressure to begin exactly as announced is just not there. In today's international business environment some Koreans make adjustments to the Western penchant for punctuality, but remember, while working in Korea, a Westerner is more likely to encounter the Korean manner and use of time.

To Koreans, Westerners often appear pre-occupied with time. Americans in particular, specify time in conversation more frequently than Koreans, for example, "I'll be back in ten minutes" or wait a "minute" as opposed to the Korean "please wait" or "wait a moment". In a typically busy Western lifestyle we frequently "have no time" or ask please "give me time". Westerners seem forever in a rush and the old saying "he who hesitates is lost", appears to be the rule. Western life appears dominated by time, a definite contrast to the somewhat patient approach to life more commonly found in Korea. Of course, those who live in busy cities like Seoul may argue the pace of life and treatment of time are no different than in the West. A closer look however, will still reveal, in many situations, the traditional Korean approach to time.

AGE — AN IMPORTANT DISCRIMINATOR

In a strictly hierarchical society numerous factors come to distinguish status and privilege. By Confucian standards age is one of the important discriminators. Respect for elders is integral to Korean society. Elderly persons receive special treatment and are afforded many more privileges than mere senior citizen discounts. Age as a distinguishing factor is not limited to the elderly, but applies to persons at all levels of society. Throughout their lives Koreans must acknowledge, and defer to, persons even slightly older than themselves and will be acknowledged by others if they are the elder. In the context of Korean business, it is difficult for two people of dissimilar age to work together as equals. For this reason consider matching persons of similar age, when possible, to more easily maintain harmony. If not, substitute some other distinguishing factor to compensate for differences in age such as education, position, or wealth. It becomes especially relevant when aggressive young foreign representatives are assigned to deal with much older Korean counterparts. The younger persons may be intimidated or dominated by the older ones. The young employees may also be rendered ineffective if the older clients refuse to accept them and limit productive contact. Sometimes younger foreigners fail to show the level of respect older Koreans expect and this may strain a business relationship. Determine in advance the age of potential contacts in Korean companies, and consider age when assigning duties or planning future relationships.

It may be surprising to learn that age is calculated differently in Korea than in the West. For example, if a Korean claims to be 29 he is really 28 by Western standards. To explain the difference one might say that in the West, years of age are counted and in Korea, birthdays are counted. In effect, at birth a person is one as that is the first birthday. One year later, that person is two, and so on, counting age much the same way Westerners count centuries.

NAMES — THE ORIENTAL VIEW

In the Orient, custom dictates that personal names are written in order of family name, first name and middle name and with few exceptions names will contain three syllables. So the name Kim Jong-ho refers to Mr. Kim. It may appear written in English in a couple of variations including a comma after the family name but the most common and easily understood form is the one as written above with a hyphen between the given and middle names. Confusion may result when meeting certain Koreans who deal frequently with Westerners or have lived abroad. Some of them have adopted the Western custom of writing names with the given name first, and so in the example above, it's possible to receive a business card that says Jong-ho Kim. If meeting for the first time a foreigner might mistakenly think he is Mr. Jong. Don't worry though as this is by far the exception. Take care to get the name correct early as it is embarrassing to mistake names.

While it may not be readily apparent, many Korean names take on different looks when translated into English. Names such as Lee, Rhee, Yi, Yee, Li, all come from the same Korean derivative pronounced more like "EE". Koreans often try to spell their name in English in such a way as to make it easier for foreigners to pronounce it correctly. As a result Pak becomes Park, to preclude pronunciation as "pack".

It won't take long to discover there are an extraordinary number of Kim's, Lee's and Pak's in this country. Astoundingly, the three names combined constitute about 44% of the population broken down as Kim 21%, Lee 14.8%, and Pak 8.5%. Of course these three names are a small portion of the total family names in existence. In all, there are well over 150 other names including fairly common ones such as Choi, Chung, Shin, Im, Paek, Kang, and Chang etc.

Remember that names are very personal to Koreans and are usually not used in conversation. Westerners generally feel more comfortable using first names and often consider it a sign of friendship. Westerners may be tempted to develop a "first-name basis" with Korean business contacts to feel secure in the relationship. DO NOT practice this in Korea. First names are rarely used and most often only between very close friends in certain circumstances. Position names or titles are very common and are used in place of personal names (director, doctor, general, uncle, etc.). Most positions have a corresponding title that may be used in conversation. Even family members have terms to label their relative positions such as oldest brother, younger sister, cousin etc., and individuals will likely be referred to by this label, as opposed to their given names. Even in marriage, names are rarely used between spouses, substituting a nickname or such to call each other. When conversing with unfamiliar persons the word teacher, pronounced Son Saeng Nim, is a kind of cover-all reference, especially when speaking to an elder, as it acknowledges respect for the person's age and status. A teacher in Korea, occupies a respected position and is given special deference within the language. The title, teacher, can also be used in conjunction with a family name, for example, Lee Son Saeng Nim.

During conversation don't be afraid to omit a name altogether. Actually, with a little practice, people can easily converse without referring to each other by name. This is the safest method especially if the two are not familiar with each other or are unsure of one another's position or title. If this is too difficult to master, try using a position title and last name only like, Director Kim, Doctor Lee, etc., but never just the last name, for example "Hey Kim", as it is considered rude and can quickly spoil a relationship. In general, a foreigner can safely use the term Mister, combined with a last name, but when meeting persons of much higher rank, Mister Kim, for example, may not signify enough respect and might be considered impolite. In Western culture, when meeting a President, Ambassador, Senator, Judge etc., it is preferable to address them as Judge Jones rather than Mr. Jones etc. The same courtesy applies in Korea, but to an even greater degree.

Also remember that the rule for Mister does not apply to Mrs. Women retain their maiden name after marriage so Mr. Kim's wife is not Mrs. Kim. She is normally referred to as the wife of Mr. Kim (there are specific Korean terms for it). The terms vary and become more significant if the woman is the boss's wife or the wife of a high ranking individual. Before becoming frustrated or discouraged by the complexity, remember foreigners are relatively safe not referring to wives at all by name, but speaking as described above. If a foreigner is unsure, but wants to show proper respect, it is always acceptable to use the term teacher as explained above. It is generally acceptable to use Miss when addressing unmarried women although there is a specific term for them in Korean (*Agassi*).

One last tip, never write a person's name in red. It is reserved for the dead and considered impolite.

PERSONAL APPEARANCE
— CAN MAKE A SIGNIFICANT IMPACT

Reportedly, Confucius once said, "Clothes distinguish a cultured man from a barbarian." Koreans take personal appearance seriously and are deeply concerned about theirs - it's a status maker. The way people look, act and even smell have a significant impact on others, regardless of culture. Foreign businessmen are advised to ensure their appearance reflects the image they want to project. Especially for a foreigner, clothes are one important factor defining the overall image. That image should reflect status and dignity. Proper image can either open or close doors of opportunity so Westerners are wise to ensure their image opens them. Dress well and conservatively at all times. Avoid casual American style (jeans, T-shirts) unless specifically encouraged to wear, like during a company picnic etc. Koreans often dress for parties, picnics, trips to the zoo, or other casual functions, in shirts and slacks, even suits, so control the temptation to dress informally. Also, avoid loud colors and prints that standout or stray too much from the mainstream. Although foreigners are allowed some leeway, the objective is to win friends so don't cash in those foreigner "chips" unnecessarily. Stick to darker colors and mainstream business styles. Save the more individually expressive garments for home.

FAMILY VALUES — THE GLUE OF SOCIETY

Still the basis of harmony in Korean society, the family binds the entire society together. The stoic father figure as head of household and the educated but reserved home-centered wife are the nucleus. If grandparents are living they also play an important role in guiding the family often residing in the same household. Such a homespun role may seem a bit ironic given that the father usually works long hours and then spends considerable time drinking with friends to fulfill obligations of his social network. Somehow however, he fulfills family obligations,doing his part to carry on the traditions. Confucian principles dictate strict guidelines and responsibilities for family members. Each member occupies a place in a distinct hierarchy and specific titles label each position. Sons in particular play an important role in the family and are still prized and favored by parents. Among sons, the eldest bears the most responsibility and enjoys the most privileges. He is essentially responsible for the welfare of the family and normally inherits most of the family fortune along with the considerable responsibility of performing traditional family rituals and caring for other family members. Wives become part of the husband's family upon marriage although they retain their maiden name. Wives are much more influential than Westerners usually assume. In fact, their power within the family is considerable and should not be underestimated. Wives and families are traditionally not included in business-related social functions although there are exceptions and a Western trend seems to be developing. Koreans keep detailed records of family histories and often maintain close relations with distant relatives. Such family networks contribute to their success and one family member will often share good fortune with other relatives in some way.

EDUCATION — TIME HONORED AND RESPECTED

Confucian teachings emphasize and esteem education. Koreans sincerely respect educated people and hold teachers in especially high regard. Teachers are so well respected that where Westerners use Mister, Koreans substitute teacher, as a term of respect which applies to both male and female. Higher education is a great social forge where individuals meet friends and cement relationships that will last their entire life. In fact, a large part of college life is spent developing this bonding process sometimes at the expense of actual studies. Where a person attended school is also significant. The most prestigious university in modern Korea has long been Seoul National University. It is the most difficult to enter and alumni usually secure important positions in government and business after graduation. Once there, they tend to support their former school by hiring and promoting other alumni. Other top schools such as Korea University and Yonsei University have similar connections. Of the scores of other universities, the most respected ones are in Seoul and schools located in the provinces are viewed as slightly less prestigious. As a foreigner functioning in this environment what matters most is to know these distinctions exist and how to capitalize on them. Undoubtedly, some Korean employees or contacts may be able to assist through their established network of friends or alumni. Don't underestimate the power of these groups. They can be very helpful in facilitating introductions and actually contributing to successful business operations.

Korea's educational system is a bit different than that of the West. From early school years, Korean students learn most of their lessons, as they did in the old Confucian system, by rote memory. Students have little opportunity to ask probing questions or inquire why; instead they listen, take notes and memorize. Some argue this system produces fewer creative thinkers, that learning without curiosity results in students who can't think on their own. Regardless of whether it's true, understand their education was formed much differently than those educated in the West. This system is slowly changing but will likely remain, in some similar form, for generations.

RELIGION — BREAKING SOME OLD MYTHS

Many Westerners arrive in Korea assuming most Koreans are Buddhist. This is far from the reality. In fact, there are almost as many Christians here as Buddhists. The more interesting truth is a large percentage of Koreans are eclectic, combining portions of several faiths. An even larger percentage claim allegiance to no specific religion. Statistics in 1991 revealed the breakdown of major religions in Korea as follows:

Buddhism		23.7%
Christians		21.1%
	(Protestants	16.3%)
	(Catholics	4.8%)
Confucian		1.5%
Others		0.8%
No Religion		52.9%

Buddhism - Introduced to Korea in 392 AD from China, it spread rapidly throughout the peninsula. It thrived during the Koryo Dynasty (936-1392) when the founder of Koryo, Wanggon, designated it the national religion. Thousands of temples were constructed and monasteries were filled to capacity with monks. The following Yi Dynasty (1392-1910) opted to reinstate and promote Confucianism and ultimately suppressed Buddhism.

Christianity - Catholic missionaries arrived first, in Korea, and by the mid nineteenth century had converted a sizable group of loyal followers. Because of conflicts between Catholicism and Confucianism, among other reasons, serious persecutions of Catholics occurred, in the early to mid 1800's resulting in thousands of deaths, many by beheading. Protestant missionaries arrived in the late nineteenth century and have flourished in Korea.

Confucianism - Like Buddhism, Confucianism also arrived in Korea in the fourth century. It was later adopted as the state religion for over five hundred years of the Yi Dynasty. Although it lacks a deity to worship, Confucianism provides strict moral guidelines for conduct between individuals and relationships within society. It strongly emphasizes education, ancestor worship and respect for elders. Although practiced as a religion by only a small number of citizens today, its influence is evident in almost all aspects of Korean society. Much of the etiquette and ritual in the Korean social system is derived from Confucianism. The honorifics and multiple expressions of respect in the language are directly related to it. The family system and various other aspects of everyday life have all been influenced by Confucianism. Learn as much about Confucianism as possible and refer to it as the origin of why some Korean customs are different from those in the West.

Followers of other faiths such as Islam and Korean indigenous religions exist in smaller numbers. Korea is a country rich in diverse religious beliefs with a core of Confucianism woven into the fabric of the nation.

REGIONALISM
— UNDERSTANDING LOCAL PREJUDICE

As a rule, foreigners should never become involved in local prejudices but knowing about them can help explain a few of the riddles of Korean life and help foreigners avoid some traps that can cause social trouble. Like any country, prejudice is deeper in some geographic areas than others and underlying bad feelings can affect office relationships and productivity. Korea is no exception. Local prejudices are based on region and social status,not race, and the associated emotions can run deep.

Some notable animosity exists between the provinces of Chollado and Kyongsangdo. A more than friendly rivalry exists between these provinces which can probably be traced to the Three Kingdoms period early in Korean history. Most recently, Chollado residents have felt left out of Korea's modern economic growth and political development. Disappointment was accentuated by the fact that the last four presidents were born in Kyongsangdo and much of Korea's so-called economic miracle appeared to have benefitted people from that region. There are prejudices between the other provinces as well but they are noticeably less pronounced.

Once again, recognize local prejudices without contributing to them. If at all possible, refrain from negatively commenting on any specific area or town. To accidentally offend someone, from a certain hometown or nearby area, would be disastrous and difficult to recover from.

Another form of social prejudice exists, between those of differing social status, which may trace its origins to the old Yi Dynasty social class system of *Yangban* and *Ssangnom*. The *Yangban* were the educated upper class with almost exclusive access to power, wealth and important government positions. The *Ssangnom* occupied the lower class, mostly uneducated and forced to perform all types of menial labor. Even today, those employed as a butcher, undertaker, garbage man, and entertainer to name a few, carry a social stigma that has persisted since the Yi Dynasty. Another bit of contrast between Korean and American culture here. All kinds of labor is respected in America, and hard work is esteemed. Individuals are expected to work hard, and be proud of their labors, it's part of the Puritan work ethic. As Alexis de Toqueville described in *Democracy in America*, over 150 years ago, "The notion of labor is presented to the mind on every side as the necessary natural and honest condition of human existence." Americans work around the house, fix their own cars, do odd jobs, and a variety of other such chores. Americans like to "pitch in" especially to help friends or colleagues. Hard work is the pride of America and rags-to-riches stories are the American dream. Koreans however, view manual labor as demeaning, an indicator of lower class. They are very hard workers, make no mistake, but they view manual labor differently from Westerners, and they esteem academic pursuits and accomplishments much more. A foreigner should keep this in mind when discussing his background and comparing family stories. It may not be wise to proudly tell a story of growing up poor and gaining wealth through manual labor. Such an accomplishment may not be appreciated as much as back home.

LUNAR CALENDAR — STILL USEFUL

Koreans did not adopt the Gregorian, or solar, calendar until King Kojong ordered so in the late 19th century. Therefore most important historical dates are listed by the lunar calendar. Westerners should also remember that quite a few Koreans still celebrate their birthdays by the lunar calendar. One embarrassed foreigner planned to surprise a Korean friend with a birthday gift only to discover that his birthday had already passed and was celebrated according to the lunar calendar. Westerners should be sure to select the correct date by the proper calendar to prevent similar embarrassment. In addition, some major holidays are still celebrated by the lunar calendar. The two most important are the lunar New Year and Chusok. Lunar New year (1 January by the lunar calendar) can fall anywhere in January or February by the solar calendar. It is celebrated throughout the Orient and is a time of great festivity. Korean families come together and pay homage to their ancestors during this special time. The solar New Year has also gained popularity and is celebrated much the same as in the West.

Chusok, (15 August by the lunar calendar) is an Autumn festival, most often compared with American Thanksgiving. Usually falling sometime in August or September by the solar calendar, this holiday is a popular time for relatives to return to their hometown to visit with their extended families and pay respect to their ancestors. It is also a popular gift-giving period and smart businessmen take advantage of this holiday to present small gifts to close Korean associates. Fruit, meats, and alcohol may all be given during Chusok. Department stores also offer additional gift suggestions including pre-packed gift boxes suitable for holiday giving.

ORIENTAL ZODIAC
— SUPERSTITION OR GUIDEPOST?

Derived from the ancient Chinese study of the sun the Oriental Zodiac plays a significant part in the lives of Koreans. The zodiac is divided into twelve parts each named for a separate animal. Each year is associated with one of the animals and so Koreans often ask the sign (*tti*) of another. From that they can determine the year that person was born. With other information such as month, day and hour of birth, fortune tellers can explain much about an individual's personality, past history and even the future. The order of the twelve animals and some sample corresponding years are as follows:

Rat : 1936, 1948, 1960, 1972, 1984
Ox : 1937, 1949, 1961, 1973, 1985
Tiger : 1938, 1950, 1962, 1974, 1986
Rabbit : 1939, 1951, 1963, 1975, 1987
Dragon : 1940, 1952, 1964, 1976, 1988
Snake : 1941, 1953, 1965, 1977, 1989
Horse : 1942, 1954, 1966, 1978, 1990
Sheep : 1943, 1955, 1967, 1979, 1991
Monkey: 1944, 1956, 1968, 1980, 1992
Chicken: 1945, 1957, 1969, 1981, 1993
Dog : 1946, 1958, 1970, 1982, 1994
Boar : 1947, 1959, 1971, 1983, 1995

〈12 Animals of the Oriental Zodiac〉

Of course, similar to the Western Zodiac, people born under certain signs are said to possess certain personality characteristics and are more compatible with people from other specific signs. This can be fun for Westerners to compare but Koreans take it more seriously. Important events of everyday life such as weddings, the birth of a child, moving to a new home, starting a business or journey, and a host of other events are often determined after consulting a fortune teller. One extreme example appeared in 1991 as the 27th of October was deemed a "propitious day" according to this system. Such a day only occurs once every sixty years and scores of thousands of people rushed to take advantage of it. Airports were so overwhelmed with travelers they were forced to call in emergency help. Wedding halls were bursting with couples trying to marry. Movers were swamped with requests for services that day and hospitals and clinics were even full of women wanting to deliver their children on that lucky day. With this in mind it's easier to see the significance of this system in the lives of everyday people. Understanding a little about the Oriental Zodiac will help foreigners understand more about Korea and the psyche of the wonderful people who live there.

Considering the role of both the lunar calendar and the Oriental Zodiac there are a few days in a person's life that are of great importance and a time of great celebration; the hundredth day of life, the first birthday, marriage, and the 60th birthday. When a baby reaches its first one hundred days, a special ceremony (baek-il) is given in its honor. Since the first few months of infancy were traditionally the most vulnerable period for a baby's health,this celebration has always been a happy time for family and friends to enjoy the progress of an infant's development. If invited to the party, guests should bring a small gift, usually baby clothes are appropriate. When the first birthday actually arrives, another ceremony, (chot tol), is prepared. Family and friends are invited, plenty of food is provided, and a good time is had by all. This is also the time when the baby is allowed to symbolically predict his own future. Various items such as a book, a pen, money, and thread, are assembled before the child. Each one has a special meaning and the item the child chooses first will determine its destiny. The money means wealth, the pen a career as a writer, the book means scholarly pursuits, thread means long life. The ceremony is an interesting and colorful part of Korean customs.

Marriage is an important day in almost any culture. It's a happy time for parents and family as well as the bride and groom. If invited, foreigners should participate in the festivities. A gift of cash is always appreciated and should be provided in a white envelope to those at the ceremony designated to collect the gifts. The 60th birthday (*hwangap*) is the new beginning in the cycle of life. Every year in the Oriental calendar has a name and when the twelve-year cycle is repeated five times the cycle of life is complete and a new one begins. The *Hwangap*, is a festive time when friends and relatives gather to celebrate this achievement. There is much eating, drinking, singing and dancing. It is an honor for foreigners to be invited and they should take advantage of the opportunity by joining in the celebrations. Foreigners living and working in Korea are likely to have a friend, employee or relative of such a person celebrating one of these special days. Take the time to share this happy time with them.

KOREAN HOLIDAYS — BE PART OF THE FUN

There are twelve national holidays, and scores of festivals during the year and each one provides a break from the routine and a welcome chance to relax. In addition, holidays may present an excellent opportunity for Westerners to strengthen the personal bond with their Korean business counterparts by either remembering to present a small gift or actually sharing in the festivities if invited. Remember, three of the holidays are determined by the lunar calendar so their dates change every year. Some holidays are marked by parades and public celebrations for all to enjoy and others are more private family celebrations. Try to learn something about each holiday and how you might enjoy experiencing it.

New Year's Day - Celebrated the first two days of the

new year. Families gather from all over and spend time together. They enjoy various traditional foods and play traditional Korean games. Photo opportunities abound as family members often wear their bright and colorful traditional clothes. Younger family members pay respect to their elders by bowing to their grandparents or parents. These activities were exclusively celebrated on the traditional lunar New Year's day but some have adjusted them to coincide with the solar calendar. One note: Koreans do not celebrate New Year's Eve exactly as in the West. New Year's Eve celebrations, common in the West, are not held during that period. In December, however, Koreans do throw end-of-year parties to celebrate the outgoing year. There is one interesting tradition which does occur on New Year's Eve. Thousands of people gather in downtown Seoul at Poshingak, a large two story pavilion housing a great bell. At midnight on New Year's Eve, the bell is rung 33 times to bring in the new year. Poshingak is located on the corner of Chongno and Namdaemunno. The streets are closed to vehicles, during that period, and throngs of people enjoy the festive atmosphere there. (1 January)

Lunar New Year - It was known for a short while in Korea as Folklore Day, or what some in the West call the Chinese New Year. Of course this holiday is determined by the lunar calendar and may fall anywhere in January or February by the solar calendar. Most families still celebrate this holiday in the traditional fashion. Families gather from all over and pay homage to their elders and ancestors. It is a wonderful and colorful family holiday.

Independence Day - Korea suffered under Japanese colonial rule from 1910-1945. In 1919, some courageous patriots declared independence from Japan by reading a prepared statement in Pagoda Park in downtown Seoul. The declaration sparked a nation-wide movement to struggle against Japanese rule. Every year on

Independence Day, the declaration is read at Pagoda Park in memory of this historic moment. (1 March)

Arbor Day - During Japanese colonial rule,Korea lost many of its natural resources including most of its timber. People of all ages participate in the reforestation of the country by planting and caring for trees. (5 April)

Buddha's Birthday - A very popular and colorful holiday, celebrations are usually held at Buddhist temples around the peninsula. The highlight of festivities is the huge lantern parade which starts at Youido Island in Seoul and ends at Chogye Temple in the downtown area. The parade features many brightly colored floats and lotus lanterns. At Chogye Temple, the decorations are extensive and perfect for photos. Visitors are welcome but remember it is a religious celebration and not staged as a tourist attraction. Determined by the lunar calendar (8 April), it may fall anywhere in April or May by the solar calendar.

Children's Day - The nation's children have their way on this wonderful holiday. Amusement parks and other children's facilities are overloaded with kids and their families all having a good time. Originally promoted to advance the health and happiness of children, this day has developed into a major holiday. (5 May)

Memorial Day - Honoring the nation's war dead, this solemn holiday features many memorial services and wreath-laying ceremonies especially at national cemeteries. (6 June)

Constitution Day - After the liberation of Japan at the close of World War II, a new government was formed. This day commemorates the institution of the new constitution in 1948. (17 July)

Liberation Day - In memory of the joyous liberation from thirty five years of Japanese colonial rule at the end of World War II. (15 August)

Chusok - Arguably the most important holiday in the country, some call it the Thanksgiving of Korea. From wherever they have scattered, relatives attempt to return to their hometown to visit with each other and worship their ancestors. Usually a three-day holiday, it falls on 15 August by the lunar calendar which is sometime in August or September by the solar calendar.

National Foundation Day - According to legend, the first Korean kingdom was founded in 2333 B.C. by the legendary figure known as Tangun. The nation remembers its original roots on this national holiday.
(3 October)

Christmas - Celebrated much the same way as Western countries, religious ceremonies, Christmas T.V. specials and department store sales and decorations abound.
(25 December)

Other holidays may sound familiar to Westerners but are celebrated a little differently. The following additional holidays are noteworthy but not celebrated as national holidays.

Valentines Day - In Korea, this is generally a day when females give chocolates to special male friends. Men may reciprocate the following month on White Day (14 March) when males provide peppermint candies to women they wish to woo. (14 February)

Parents' Day - Whereas some countries celebrate separate holidays for both mothers and fathers, Koreans combine the two and celebrate it as Parents' Day.
(8 May)

Armed Forces Day - Honoring the Armed Forces of the Republic of Korea, this day was usually marked by a huge parade, through downtown Seoul, including tanks, planes, trucks and military personnel from all branches of the service. In recent years the parade has been limited to once every three years. Foreigners in country during this period are encouraged to see this extravaganza. The parade is colorful and entertaining. (1 October)

Korean Alphabet Day - Honoring the development of the Korean alphabet (*Hangul*), which was originated by a group of scholars under direction of the wise King Sejong. The alphabet was ultimately presented to the people in 1446. Koreans are rightfully proud of *Hangul* and set aside this day to commemorate its beginning and promote its development. Various cultural seminars and concerts are usually held to help celebrate the holiday. (9 October)

OJANG — SEALS INSTEAD OF SIGNATURES

Even in the West, in ancient times seals were used to identify persons or add authenticity to official documents. It seems seals have always been quite ornamental and creatively designed. Of course we still use some seals in a very limited sense today, mostly decorative, but such seals have all but disappeared in the West, having been replaced by the signature, for identification purposes. In the Orient however, especially in Korea and China, seals are still used as a means of identification, authentication and decoration. In Korea, these seals are called "*tojang*" and are usually hand-carved and still quite ornamental. Each one is as individual and important as a signature in the West. *Tojang* are required on all official documents, and artists almost always use a more decorative style to authenticate their works. It is common to hear them referred to as a "chop" but that term is not Korean and is unknown to all but foreigners. *Tojang* were traditionally carved from soapstone or wood but modern plastic is also common today. The tip of the *tojang* must be dipped in a kind of pasty red ink before applying it to a document. This ink is typically kept in a small tray, or other container, commonly found on the desk in an office. This unique tradition continues in Korea.

THAT OPPOSITE CULTURE

There are many cultural differences where East meets West on the Korean peninsula. In many ways, the differences are so great they are actually opposite. This causes considerable confusion, and often frustration for foreigners who often find the customs, methods, and culture so difficult to understand. The problem for foreigners may lay in the expectation that Korea will somehow be similar to their own country, and when faced with the stark differences, dramatic confusion and frustration results. The foreknowledge that Korean culture is opposite in many ways should create a new expectation that will result in understanding without judgement and allow smoother relations and cooperation between foreigners and their Korean hosts.

Mentioned below are a few examples of the many contrasts one may encounter in Korea. Some are very basic, some a little humorous, but they touch very diverse aspects of life and are intended to invite Westerners to think a little differently, not only when they look at these examples, but when they encounter the countless others while visiting and working in Korea.

Individual vs. Group - As mentioned earlier in this Chapter,Westerners, especially Americans, place more emphasis on individualism, teaching their children to become independent from an early age. Koreans are reared with group values, carefully reinforced and interwoven into their culture throughout their entire lives.

Written Text - Traditional Korean books read back to
front, right to left in lines written vertically. Western
books read front to back, left to right in lines written
horizontally. Modern books read like Western ones
but Korean newspapers generally read vertically.

Addresses - Western addresses read from the individual
to the smallest unit (street) to the largest unit
(state), written horizontally on the envelope. Korean
addresses read from the largest unit (province) to
the smallest (house) and the person is listed last.
The addresses were once written vertically on the
envelope but this custom has slowly disappeared.

Bells - Westerners are most familiar with bells with the
clapper mounted inside. They often ring large bells

by moving them back and forth allowing the clapper to rattle the inside. Korean bells are stationary, and suspended from overhead, with the clapper on the outside. To ring it they swing the clapper, also usually suspended from overhead, striking the side of the bell from the outside.

Names - Oriental names list the family name first, followed by first and middle names. Western names list in order of first, middle and last name.

Titles - In the West, titles are normally placed first in conversation, for example, Doctor Smith, Mister Jones, or President Bush. Koreans place titles after the name, for example Smith Paksa (doctor), Bush Dae Tong Nyong (president).

Directions - Westerners list directions; north, south east, west, but Koreans list them east, west, south, north.

Waving - In the West, if a person holds up their hand, palm out, and moves their fingers up and down they would be waving goodbye. In Korea, they would be calling you to "come here."

5 Days 4 Nights - In the West, especially in English, they say the number of days first but in Korea nights are first, for example, 4 nights 5 days.

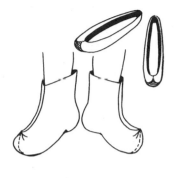

Shoes and Socks - Traditional Korean footwear has left and right socks and shoes that fit either foot. You know Western footwear has left and right shoes with socks that fit either foot.

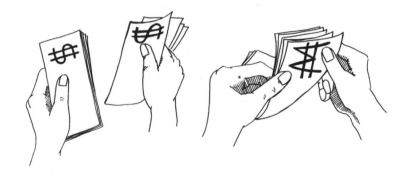

Counting Money - Koreans count money by folding a group of bills tightly in the left hand and flipping through the bills with the fingers of the opposite hand. Westerners count them one at a time by separating each bill as they count and placing it on a table or other flat surface.

Eating Habits - In the West, people go to great length to eat and chew without making noise. Koreans may sometimes slurp their soup and smack their lips while enjoying a meal.

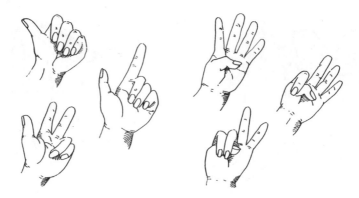

Counting on Your Fingers - Most Westerners are familiar with counting on their fingers. Western culture dictates starting with a closed fist and counting 1,2,3,4,5 as the hand opens first with the thumb, then index finger, middle finger, etc., finally end with a completely open hand at the number 5. Koreans begin with an open hand and count by closing all the digits, beginning with the thumb, and ending with a closed hand at number 5.

Sidewalks - Most people in the West walk down the right side of the sidewalk, but in Korea they walk down the left.

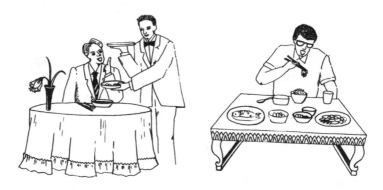

Meals - Foreigners are probably accustomed to meals served in courses one after the other, for example, soup, salad, main course, etc., but Koreans serve the complete meal at once in many dishes, to the group, and guests may choose from all the dishes as a group.

Carrying Loads - Generally, in the West people carry all sorts of items, be it groceries, children, boxes, etc., in front of them as they walk. Koreans generally carry items on their back making the load easier and allowing more unobstructed vision. Korean mothers can often be seen carrying infants on their back, kind of papoose or Indian style.

Suntans - In the West, a tan body is desirable and a sign of health and youth. An entire industry caters to sunbathers who spend much money and many hours attempting to darken their skin. Koreans favor fair skin and some women go to great lengths to shield their skin from the sun. Many women who must spend much time outdoors will attempt to shade themselves from the tanning rays of the sun

Laughing - Westerners laugh with their mouths open often making great noise and even doubling over while holding their stomach. Koreans, especially women, cover their mouths while laughing attempting not to show their teeth or act over emotional.

Emergency Numbers - Almost everyone is familiar with the emergency telephone number, 911, in America. It has even spawned a popular T.V. show of the same name. Even this simple part of everyday life appears reversed in Korea, for as you have probably guessed, their emergency telephone number is 119.

See how many others you can recognize during your Korean experience.

4

INTERPERSONAL BUSINESS RELATIONS

INTRODUCTIONS
— THE SMART WAY TO MAKE CONTACT

While Westerners are generally outgoing and often willing to introduce themselves to prospective clients, this approach is the least effective way to initiate contact in Korea. Third party introductions are the universally accepted and approved way to meet new acquaintances or gain initial access to a company. This delicate process should not be approached casually. It's imperative that the right person at the proper level within a company make the introduction. Gaining access either too low or too high in the bureaucracy can cause future difficulty. In general, introductions are made most effectively in person. Don't be tempted to conduct such an important formality by telephone. Especially early in relationship development, face-to-face contact is preferable. It is normal to mix business with pleasure, during initial meetings, but utilizing continuous personal contact is definitely an advantage. Of course common sense also applies. Insisting on personal meetings in every situation is usually unworkable and could label you a nuisance. Always maintain personal contact without overdoing it for the best results.

Also know that Koreans take certain introductions personally. They are not quick to casually introduce one another nor inclined to introduce without permission. While walking with a Korean friend and a third party is met, the Korean may not introduce the third party to the foreigner. He may stop and talk for a short while seemingly leaving the foreigner out of the conversation. This is not impolite. The foreigner should just stand by patiently until he is through. In a similar situation, if a foreigner meets a third party on the street, he shouldn't be too anxious to introduce a Korean friend. The Korean may not want to meet the person and an introduction may be awkward for him. Western custom prescribes introducing a third party at the risk of being impolite but Korean custom is not so. Foreigners encountering a third party under these circumstances should just exchange brief greetings, small talk, etc., with the third party and continue on with the Korean friend. No one will be offended by the encounter.

THAT FIRST MEETING
— MAKING A GOOD IMPRESSION

That first face-to-face meeting can have a serious long term effect on building a successful relationship. Expend every effort to ensure the meeting results in a lasting positive impression on the Koreans involved. Keeping the following few small tips in mind should produce the desired result.

Dress Well - The first visual impression someone receives is based on how people look and dress. Even in the first few seconds, before exchanging greetings, an impression begins forming in the other person's mind based largely on appearance. Throughout the meeting that impression expands and solidifies as closer examination permits. Often, the initial impression is reinforced as the interview progresses and, if the first impression was negative, it is difficult to reverse. Fortunately, individuals have the ability to greatly influence a first impression by preparing to look their best (see Appearance). Westerners should dress to impress, but not to overwhelm. Conservative well-made suits for men, conservative well-made attractive outfits for women are always the smart choice.

Greeting - Traditionally Koreans met each other with bows. This custom still flourishes but the Western handshake has also been added. Foreigners are not expected to bow but the foreigner who does will likely win the respect of the host. When shaking hands try not overdo it with high arm pumping maneuvers. A firm hand shake with one or two hands is most appropriate but refrain from the old vicegrip. Koreans are not impressed by a Western display of overpowering hand strength. If introduced to a female a slight bow is usually enough but be prepared to shake hands if she desires. With females a gentler handshake is appropriate.

Business Cards - Carry a full supply of cards at all times as excellent contact opportunities frequently appear unexpectedly. Offer a business card with both hands and a slight bow. Try to exchange cards while standing,

United Life Insurance

Bernard Richie
Vice President

113-25 Samsung-dong
Kangnam-gu, Seoul
135-100, Korea
Tel:822)734-5087
Fax:822)730-8192

United Life Insurance

Bernard Richie
副社長

135-100
서울特別市 江南區
三星洞 113-25
Tel:822)734-5087
Fax:822)730-8192

for a better impression, and receive cards in the same way. Try not to study the card at that time. Glance at it, glean the most important information such as name and position, and put the card away. An attractive and well designed card is highly encouraged. Ensure it has both English and Korean versions printed on the same or opposite sides. Consider adding some prestige to the card, especially when dealing with high ranking Koreans, by using *Hanmun* (Chinese characters) in certain portions of the Korean translation of the personal I.D. such as title, company name and contact information. *Hanmun* may be a little inconvenient for some common Koreans to decipher, so determine the value and extent of this option for your particular purpose. For example, using *Hanmun* in translating the name only may be appropriate.

Listen Attentively - Be an active listener! It is very uncomfortable, and difficult to have a meaningful meeting if one member looks tired or seems disinterested. Coversations can sometimes grow tiresome if working through an interpretor. Look at the Korean when he speaks, nod, smile, moan, anything to let him know you're truly following the conversation. Laugh when he laughs, smile when he smiles, but be careful not to overdo it. If a hearty laugh is not appropriate, don't fake it, try a smile and some approving head nods instead. Foreigners should try their best to look sincere, if a Korean suspects insincerity, distrust may begin and the relationship will suffer. Don't interrupt the conversation especially if the other person is an elder. Let the other person finish speaking. Even those who love to talk will eventually allow time for others to interject. Some people are naturally slow talkers and take more time to compose their thoughts, especially in a foreign language. Interrupting them may offend. Don't fear silence, give others the time needed to compose themselves. Koreans are much more comfortable with silence than Westerners. They are actually more interested in maintaining a feeling of harmony that does not necessitate constant dialogue.

Speak Clearly - Foreigners should look at the person they are speaking to and speak slowly and clearly. Avoid pigeon English or baby talk, if the Korean counterpart speaks English at all he will be offended. Use simple concise sentences absent of idioms or slang. English is full of colorful expressions but they are almost impossible to translate and difficult to understand.

Pump that Kibun - If a Westerner has done his homework, he will have identified some personal commonalities that can be used as a basis for friendly discussion. Be sure to intersperse a few well-placed compliments, during the conversation, and keep smiling. Maintaining high spirits will please the Korean contact and make him comfortable. Including a small gift or a memento to commemorate the meeting can make a more positive impression. An elaborate gift is not recommended, and may create embarrassment so keep it simple and personal. When meeting at a Korean's office he will likely serve some refreshments, quite possibly juice or tea. Accept whatever is offered graciously. A guest should not refuse it even if it's not to his taste. Allow the beverage to be served to the entire group and wait to drink until the host invites everyone to begin. If the beverage is not to the guest's liking he should just drink less. Remember, what's important is to allow the group to enjoy the refreshments together.

Don't Overstay Your Welcome - Busy people always appreciate the gift of time. Schedule appointments honestly never requesting more time than needed. Conversely, if a client's schedule is full, don't try to squeeze into a fifteen-minute appointment slot if an hour is really needed. If an hour was scheduled but the business was concluded in thirty minutes, all the better. However, don't try to rush and avoid the temptation to glance at a watch or clock. Spend time developing rapport but stay alert for non-verbal signals that the Korean wants to end the meeting. Remain flexible, if the foreigner has come at a slow period and the Korean host wishes to talk more, do it. The key is to read the Korean host and flow with the mood.

Make A Pleasant Exit - Before departing, thank the Korean for his time and pledge future contact and cooperation. Always leave on a positive note even if the meeting was not successful.

DO YOUR HOMEWORK

Learn About Korea - Knowing something about the country a foreigner works in is just plain good business. In Korea, it pays even bigger dividends because the people notice and appreciate it well. Just reading this book should boost most foreigners ahead of their Western competitors, but they should not stop there. Newcomers should select an interesting aspect of Korea and delve into it. Study that aspect until becoming thoroughly knowledgeable and then search for another, repeating the process, continuously increasing overall understanding of Korea. This incremental learning approach will soon yield significant results. Carrying a larger pool of knowledge to draw from will help foreigners better relate to clients and build solid relationships more quickly. Such a steady growing process will develop any newcomer into a more informed and more attractive partner.

Learn About the Business Community - Studying the leading businsses and their top leaders. In Korea, many such leaders are well-known to the average citizen and it is wise for foreigners to know something about them and their corporations. Learn which major corporations dominate which industries, and become knowledgeable of the business environment in Korea.

Learn About the Company - Knowing a partner, and his company may seem like common sense but businessmen often overlook this important aspect. Learn as much as possible about a client's company and even something about its competitors. Dig beyond the superficial into substance. Inquire about how it's organized, how decisions are made, and where the real power and influence are situated. Read trade journals, brochures, anything to help learn facts which may facilitate more interesting discussions with Korean business contacts. A foreigner's efforts will be obvious to Koreans and quite likely a pleasantly unexpected surprise. Don't try to show off with too much knowledge or utilize controversial facts which might precipitate argument. Neither culture likes a braggart or a know-it-all. Foreigners are wise to use what they've learned by interjecting interesting information into the conversation, here and there, to demonstrate their effort to understand the local environment. It's also of benefit to know enough about one's own company to offer some non-controversial comparisons which make casual conversation more enjoyable. Small talk is an art form and mastering it can support success.

A typical scene at Korean Offices.
They usually start their work early.

Learn About Key People - Become acquainted with specific members of a partner's company before they are met. Study their family, hobbies, likes, dislikes, background, education, accomplishments, anything that will enhance the ability to relate to them and quicken the rapport-building process. Make notes for later reference and update those notes with significant events, such as weddings, birth of children, outings together etc. Eventually these notes will build into dossiers which are an invaluable tool for planning successful future meetings. As the number of clients increase and the frequency of contact multiplies, such dossiers help clear confusion concerning who's who and prevent costly mistakes pertaining to individual members. Initially, some of this information can easily be learned from friends or others in their company, other information must be gathered slowly as additional contacts occur. The key is to use every opportunity to accumulate and document that information for future use. Too many times key personal facts about important partners, that could help strengthen relationships, are forgotten because they are trusted to memory. Before meeting clients consult the dossier to refresh the memory about that person and select key facts to use in casual conversation. Try not to become too personal during conversation, but include enough detail to demonstrate a sincere interest and concern for them as a person. Remember birthdays, anniversaries, travel experiences, family sicknesses etc., and congratulate or comment as appropriate.

Shared Experience - One of the most effective ways for foreigners to build successful relationships with Koreans is by developing shared experiences that leave a positive memory with their Korean friends. Shared experiences become the foundation for solid relations so strive to create as many as possible, beginning with your first meeting. Whether it be golf matches, ski trips, picnics, hiking, drinking, lunch or just a pleasant get-together, imagination can help fashion a positive experience out of any meeting.

"COMPLIMENTING" A RELATIONSHIP

A properly placed compliment is well received in almost any culture. As a Westerner might expect, however, the customs in Korea may be a little different than back home. In general, Koreans do not lavish compliments on subordinates even for a job well done. Frequent verbal rewards are not deemed necessary to encourage workers nor is it expected by them. Foreigners have some license in this regard but should try to abide by Korean custom as closely as possible. A sincere simple expression of thanks for a job well done is perfectly appropriate and if done in moderation may save the foreigner and the subordinate possible embarrassment. The same rule of thumb applies to peers. Complimenting peers is OK but Koreans rely more on unspoken actions as a sign of pleasure or displeasure. Complimenting superiors is more acceptable in Korea than Westerners may be comfortable with. The rules of Western culture might tempt some to judge such praise as "brown-nosing". Foreign businessmen are not expected to forsake their own values in this regard but must be prepared for a different custom, where complimenting superiors is more prevalent, and should try not to make judgements based on a Western set of values alone.

It is common for Westerners to compliment about the beauty of someone else's wife. In the West, persons may mention such praise to the husband,or often, directly to the wife. Common expressions such as "You look beautiful tonight" or "Your wife is very attractive" should be avoided in Korea. Other compliments are welcome however. For example, when visiting someone's home for dinner it is common to comment on the abundance of food, how delicious it was, or the amount of effort the host expended in preparation.

While it's polite for Westerners to acknowledge a compliment with a "thank you", Koreans consider this much to forward and most often will reply to a compliment with a denial. What Westerners may consider false modesty Koreans consider proper humility.

CRITICISM
— MAKING A POINT WITHOUT MAKING TROUBLE

Individuals regardless of culture are often sensitive to any of the various forms of criticism. Some contend Koreans are more sensitive to negatives about their country or culture. Be especially careful not to trip up in this area, but also tread lightly when pointing out negatives in other areas. Americans prefer straight talk, direct and to the point (except for politicians). Koreans, however, rarely appreciate frank criticism. As a rule, foreigners should avoid criticism if at all possible, but if it's unavoidable, an indirect approach is almost always better. The best indirect approach is via a third party. Koreans generally favor third parties acting as intermediaries as it more easily allows all parties to save face. In general, they would prefer not to confront problems openly or with conflict. Third parties are most effective when known by both sides. This is different than in the West where disinterested third parties are generally sought as arbitrators. It is wise to consider a third party approach first in presenting criticism. If however, criticism must be delivered personally be sure to choose the proper time when the mood is right or set the proper mood by preparing a pleasant atmosphere. Surround criticism with compliments, use an indirect approach to deliver them then, don't belabor, make the point and move on to something more pleasant, the Korean will contemplate the deeper meaning at a later time. Try not to criticize matters a Korean counterpart may already be aware of. Don't be afraid to input honest criticism if asked, but remember tact, the importance of indirect-ness, and think hard before volunteering negatives. Avoid the emotion trap by remaining calm and deliver-ing criticism with a straight face or even disguised behind a smile. The objective is to present negatives in a manner least disruptive to the receiver's *kibun*.

HUMILITY — HIGHLY DESIRABLE TRAIT

Americans value aggres-sive individual behavior, especially in business. Westerners are often impressed by the charis-matic leader, a person whose very entry into a room commands the attention of everyone pre-sent. Although modesty is valued in the West, the culture also allows room for "tooting your own horn" to get ahead if necessary. The opposite is generally the case in Korea. Respected leaders are more often humble about their accomplishments,letting others sing their praises. Instead of commanding a presence when they enter a room they are more likely to head for the lowest position at the table until others demand they move to the seat of honor or authority. This unassuming humili-ty is considered a sign of manners and good breeding. It is certainly to a foreign businessman's benefit to take a dose of humility when meeting Koreans, especially in groups. They will quickly recognize that person as a gentleman or lady, *Yangban* in Korean terms, and value them as a partner.

EMOTIONS — CONTROLLING YOURS CAN WIN FAVOR

Confucian doctrine teaches strict discipline of individual human emotions. The ability to control emotions is a sign of good breeding and maturity and an indicator of someone desirable to work with. Koreans notice how foreigners handle emotion so businessmen should be on their best behavior. Try not to visibly react to potentially emotional situations. Even a raised voice can indicate emotions taking control. Spontaneous reactions can result in embarrassing slips of the tongue. Not only the content but the fact that it was said may cause that person to lose face. Remain calm and contemplate actions and reactions carefully, especially in emotional situations. Americans respect a man who takes charge in a crisis. Remember, Korea is a group-oriented culture. If a Westerner has an aggressive personality, and feels the impulse to take charge, he has more chance of success if he does so unemotionally.

The patience of the Orient is well-known and often difficult for Westerners to adjust to. The difference in culture and the endless delays common in a Confucian bureaucracy may test a Westerner's patience. However, impatience is generally unattractive to Koreans, so remember the difference between aggressiveness and impatience. An individual may still charge hard if he does it unemotionally, but be prepared for delays. Koreans are very perceptive and will quietly observe how Westerners conduct themselves in various situations. How one treats subordinates, the waiter at lunch, or the inconsiderate driver who cut you off on the highway will all reveal something about the real self. Koreans want to know how the real self will act in a variety of situations before they commit to a relationship. Be sincere and calm. Think about what you say before you say it. Westerners would do well to present themselves as stable yet flexible, reliable and desirable to work with.

LOYALTY — UNDERSTANDING THE IMPORTANCE

Korean culture demands loyalty in various relationships. Such loyalty is derived from Confucian values that have been deeply ingrained in the society for centuries. Loyalty is paramount in relations between children and parents, individual and community, employee and employer, and between friends. Such a commitment is placed above fairness in many cases, and individuals may endure severe hardship without breaking that important bond. Within a company, persons may owe an obligation to superiors who helped in their hiring or promotion and such favors are not forgotten easily. Be sensitive to the obligations of others and try to avoid placing persons in situations that may force them to break an obligation or appear disloyal. Understand personal obligations and attend to them religiously or neglect them at the peril of your relationship and reputation. Disloyalty is a stigma that can seriously damage a reputation and ability to conduct successful business.

PERSUASION — TIMING IS EVERYTHING

Trying to convince a Korean contact to assist, if for whatever reason he is reluctant, can be tricky. One of the first moves should be to determine the source and depth of opposition. Is it philosophical or due to conflicts with his network of relationships or prior obligations? The latter will be difficult to overcome. When the time comes to make a pitch, remember, logic alone will not likely be enough to persuade. Relationships, obligations and *kibun* are all significant determinants. Once again, be sure to set the proper mood. Choose a place and time when the individual is feeling comfortable, relaxed and in good spirits. Pump that *kibun!* Be subtle with the request and be prepared to give up something small in return. Carefully consider the obligation you will incur as a result of his help. Even after all this the outcome may not be completely successful so keep an alternate plan in store.

One alternative is using third parties to influence someone a step higher in the chain than the reluctant contact. I can think of quite a few times when an individual was reluctant to assist until another friend, who happened to be a classmate of that person's boss, was contacted and a kind word was passed. The boss later relayed kind words about me to the individual which was enough to break the impasse immediately without exerting any pressure or creating hard feelings.

WORKING WITH A TRANSLATOR/INTERPRETER

One of the most important tactical business decisions a foreign businessman may make is whether to employ an interpreter. The depth of the expected business dealings in Korea will certainly be a factor in the decision to hire one, but having a personal interpreter has a few significant advantages:

- allows contact with Korean other than only those who speak English
- allows a Korean native speaker to act as an advocate
- promotes clearer and more effective translations
- provides a native cultural perspective to specific points the foreigner needs to convey

Remember, while operating on foreign turf, Westerners automatically yield certain advantages to a Korean partner or customer if they rely on another's interpreter to make their points. Also, many businesses may send an English speaker to deal with Westerners initially. This might sound convenient but the individual may not be the person the Westerner really needs to develop a relationship with in the company. The ability to communicate and relate to the right people, within a company or government agency, will greatly affect potential success. A good interpreter can learn the internal workings of a Korean company and help advise who to meet and how to relate with each person individually.

With proper training, an interpreter should do more than just translate. By understanding his employer's position better, an interpreter can describe it more clearly to the other party. He might also detect nuances which may indicate possible difficulty and will be able to advise about possible reactions to such indicators. As the Westerner's advocate, the interpreter should be better able to choose the most appropriate words to portray a particular view in the best light. Having a personal interpreter also supplies a knowledgeable guide through the maze of cultural pitfalls a foreigner may unknowingly fall into if no one is looking out for him. More important than preventing serious cultural mistakes, a good interpreter can help capitalize on cultural opportunities that could place the foreign businessman in a far more positive position, if acted on at the proper moment. Not all Koreans are well-suited for this type employment so take the time to select just the right person.

PICKING THE RIGHT INTERPRETER

Since this person can have such a serious impact on success, foreign employers should make every effort to ensure they hire the very best the company can afford. Quite a few factors are important in helping select the best choice. Remember the interpreter represents the foreign employer and the company to everyone he meets. Try to consider all the following characteristics when interviewing prospective applicants:

- Integrity
- Respectability
- Education
- Manners
- Age

- Trainablity
- Sociability
- Controllability

Integrity - Ensuring this, up front, will save much trouble in the long run. If an interpreter shows any signs of basic integrity problems he may cause difficulty at some future crucial moment when the employer least expects it or can least afford it. Investigate his reputation both before and after employment. Don't be afraid to test an interpreter's integrity periodically, without his knowledge, to ensure he is totally on the right team.

Respectability - Despite ability, if a translator has a bad reputation or makes a negative impression he will defeat the purpose of having one. Pick a respected person with a solid reputation and one with a personality that projects dignity and character.

Education - Many Koreans who speak English well may not be as well educated as they appear. They also might be good speakers but deficient in writing or other language skills. Know exactly what skills are desired and make sure to test for those skills. Many English language tests really measure listening and reading comprehension. Koreans in general are better at these skills than writing and speaking so some test scores can be deceptive. Also, their level of education will quickly become apparent when an interpreter speaks to Korean counterparts in his native language. If he is not well educated it may negatively affect his ability to be taken seriously by the counterparts. In reality, it may also affect his ability to accurately describe the Westerner's views, in just the right terms, in Korean. Nuance can clearly affect communications in several ways. If an interpreter is not professional or insensitive to nuance, resulting mistranslations can become a detractor. For example, if a Westerner wants to communicate that he would like to arrange a meeting the first of October, but the interpreter translates that he would like to arrange a meeting the "beginning of October," a problem could develop although the translation is technically correct. In this case, the intention was to communicate an exact date but the translation could be interpreted to mean the exact date was yet undetermined and may be any time in the first ten days of October. This small nuance can cost valuable time and money in delays and confusion. An untrained or non-professional interpreter can easily filter information and may also miss intended directness or emphasis which can ultimately change a meaning. Be certain an interpreter's overall education and English ability accurately matches exact needs and expectations.

Manners - Because courtesy is culturally important in Korea it is essential the interpreter, and all employees, are familiar with and employ the best manners when dealing with Korean contacts or customers. This will help diffuse any reluctance Koreans may harbor in dealing with foreigners, especially if they heard of or had any previous negative experiences in this regard. Individual Koreans do not inherit good manners by virtue of their birth. This type of polish is learned so ensure each interpreter has what it takes.

Age - Depending on how an interpreter will be used, age can be a very critical factor. If plans include using the interpreter as a negotiator or in a social setting, then the employer should certainly consider an older, experienced and dignified person. Of course if an interpreter is only needed for low level meetings or document translation then age is less of an issue. An older person, someone over 50 for example, may make high level executives more accessible and dealing with them more comfortable. Younger employees often have difficulty being accepted or gaining the proper access to older senior executives. Carefully match age with the type of work required.

Trainability - Chances are, any interpreter will have to be trained concerning the business, management style, esoteric vocabulary and many other aspects unique to working with a specific employer and company. Finding a person receptive to training is important and can prevent future difficulties. Be sure to provide specific training once employed and continuously critique and provide feedback to the interpreter concerning areas identified as needing improvement. The Westerner needs to become comfortable working with a particular interpreter and that will require training and practice.

Sociability - Especially if an interpreter will be used in any social setting, try to pick one with a personality that is socially compatible. Social graces are not inborn so don't assume every Korean has them. If an interpreter is not comfortable at parties then he may spoil the mood and ultimately the chance of success. Sometimes, an interpreter is dispatched to receive items or otherwise act in the employer's stead, so it's wise to select one that presents a good image especially in the employer's absence. A word here about female interpreters; while there are many fine female interpreters, again carefully consider exactly how the interpreter will be used before selecting one. A female interpreter will not fit in well at mostly male-only drinking parties. She also might present an awkward situation in other social settings in a mostly male dominated environment. Traveling and attending meetings together may give the wrong impression or raise unwanted suspicions of romance.

Conversely, some argue females, in general, have better English language ability and are more reliable. Remember to seriously consider these factors in the hiring decision.

Controllability - While in some circumstances a Western employer may want an interpreter who shows initiative and is somewhat outgoing, it is dangerous to select one that tends to work his own agendas or takes undue license with translations etc. Most experienced businessmen have worked with interpreters who mistranslated their meaning and later said they translated what they thought the foreigner really wanted to say. That kind of initiative can cause unnecessary problems. Some of it can be prevented with proper counseling and training sessions but some of it may be personality-driven and employers should look for indications of it early and correct it immediately. The ability to control an interpreter's actions can become crucial in negotiations and social settings.

USING AN INTERPRETER EFFECTIVELY

If a Westerner hasn't worked with an interpreter very much there are a few tips that can quickly smooth out the process and improve productivity. Most importantly, talk directly to the other person, do not talk to the interpreter. Conversation becomes awkward if the foreigner talks to the interpreter and he relays the message to the Korean. It also makes it difficult to establish rapport if the Westerner is not really conversing with the Korean. Look at the Korean throughout the conversation. This may take some effort but practice it frequently and train the interpreter in this technique from the beginning.

Secondly, make sure to speak concisely and take breaks in short enough intervals for the interpreter to effectively remember everything that was said. Otherwise, the interpreter will be forced to summarize all or part of the conversation to the best of his memory. This may also result in a poor translation as he won't have time to formulate the most appropriate vocabulary because he will be hard pressed to remember exactly what was said.

Thirdly, be careful not to speak in slang or idioms, which are likely not to translate well in Korean. Phrases like "let's get in on the ground floor," "let's call it a day,' and "play it by ear," are clear to Westerners but have no real meaning in Korean and can cause confusion. Even a better than average interpreter will likely be forced to wing it when translating them. At the very least there will be a misunderstanding, but at worst the interpreter may present a distorted meaning that could cause unnecessary confusion or even hurt the relationship with a counterpart. Also do not become impatient with an interpreter or scold him in front of counterparts. This does happen and it presents a very awkward situation and damages the status and credibility of both the foreigner and the interpreter.

Try to avoid double negatives and remember that yes to a negative question in Korean means no. For example, if asked "You don't want to go?" Yes, means "Correct, I don't want to go." In English a response might be, "No" meaning I don't want to go.

Lastly, discuss how the conversation might proceed, with the interpreter, before a scheduled meeting. This will provide an opportunity for him to raise questions concerning precise meanings and allow time to research vocabulary he may not be familiar with. After the meeting, review the discussion again and highlight words, grammar or expressions that were confusing, either translating from English to Korean or vice versa. This is also an excellent opportunity to discuss cultural mistakes made or just exchange general views on how the meeting went. It's wise to use this time to document facts about the Korean contact including bio data, likes, dislikes etc., which can help in planning future meeting.

A well-trained interpreter, used effectively, can become a real asset and a force multiplier for successful business.

AVOIDING MISUNDERSTANDINGS

Small mistakes can have grave consequences when dealing cross-culturally. Go over key points several times to eliminate confusion. Triangulate really critical points to insure accurate understanding. Describe important concepts in several different ways and even write them down if possible. Be subtle in this technique so as not to offend. A foreigner should never give the impression he thinks the Korean is stupid. Smoothly spread the triangulation over the course of the conversation. If the Korean partner is quietly listening and it's unclear if he is really in agreement, throw in a "no" question that will force his participation. An occasional question requiring a "no" response will also test his true comprehension. Another technique is to "test his limits" by making a proposal he is not likely to accept. If that doesn't spark a reaction then he may either not understand or he may be just politely agreeing with no intention of following through.

Take special care when dealing with money. It is easy to mistranslate figures from one language to another. Write down the figure and translate it more than once. Remember Western languages count money by thousands, ten thousands, hundred thousands, etc. Koreans count by ten thousands. For example, the number 100,000 is spoken as ten ten thousands, 1,000,000 is spoken as one hundred ten thousands etc. This can become very confusing between languages, especially when dealing in large figures. A foreigner may find himself dealing in such figures fairly quickly. For example, at an exchange rate of 790 won to the dollar, $10,000 = 7,900,000 won, which is spoken as 790 ten thousands. Confusion can be compounded during negotiations when many large numbers are quickly exchanged.

Also be careful with jokes, puns and sarcasm. They are often confusing or impossible to translate. If the need to use them is overpowering, keep them simple and cross-culturally understandable. Timing is often critical to a successful joke. Humor is difficult to deliver well in another language so be careful and certain of both the timing and method of delivery.

WHEN YES MEANS NO AND VICE VERSA

Koreans will often refuse food, refreshments, etc., when offered the first few times. They do so out of humbleness and courtesy and frequently wait to accept after repeated offers. Westerners often give up too soon leaving their guest wanting and frustrated. Understand this custom and continue to insist much like your grandmother likely did when you visited for dinner.

Koreans frequently agree or say yes, when they really mean no. They do so to protect another's *kibun*, as an abrupt no is considered impolite. Foreigners are expected to read this yes as conditional and understand it most likely means no. Westerners too often take the "yes" literally and are later disappointed when the outcome is not as expected. Some then go a step further and judge Koreans as unreliable because of the appearance they did not keep their word. A little knowledge of the culture can prevent misunderstanding. Westerners should lower their expectations and recheck on the agreement if the outcome is critical. Remember, pinning down a counterpart to a definite answer may make him uncomfortable. Communicating that "no" is OK while maintaining subtlety will help. "No" is best communicated politely in an indirect, indefinite way. Also keep in mind that phrasing is important. As previously mentioned, Koreans often answer "yes" to a negative question, in English, to mean "no." When we ask "You don't want to go?" If the person does not want to go we expect to hear "no." Koreans will answer "yes" to this question to indicate the same meaning. Avoid phrasing questions that lead themselves to misunderstanding.

NO VALUE JUDGEMENTS

Finally, Westerners will make a far better impression with others and feel less frustration themselves if they reserve value judgements. Just look at things, (and there will be plenty of them), as different but not crazy or stupid etc. Remember, many Korean customs have much longer histories than Western ones and have served Koreans well for thousands of years. Westerners who discover Korea with an open mind will enjoy much greater overall success.

5

BUSINESS ENTERTAINMENT

Businesses in Korea spend enormous amounts on entertainment, which is crucial to relationship development and often a strategic guarantee of trust and smooth working relations. Korean businesses spend far more on entertainment than on research and development. This may seem an odd trend but it reflects the true nature of business in Korea, something a foreigner should become acquainted with as quickly as possible to ensure success. It might be said Koreans prefer pleasure before business while Americans cling to the old saying of business before pleasure. There are many ways to entertain in Korea, a large number of which are quite different than some Westerners are accustomed to. This chapter describes some of those methods, highlighting a few of the differences which may otherwise catch a foreigner by surprise.

EATING OUT — A UNIQUE EXPERIENCE
Restaurant

Meeting with Korean counterparts over dinner is one of the most common and important methods to cement business relationships. Eating in a foreign land can be intimidating for Westerners if they are neither familiar with the food nor willing to make some adjustments to their diet. Do not fear, Korea has a wide variety of cuisine to please the most discriminating palate. Foreigners can find almost every kind of food they are accustomed to and quite a few I'm sure they have never heard of nor tasted. Selecting the right restaurant and cuisine is essential to ensuring a successful meeting. Foreign businessmen should establish themselves at a few good restaurants as a regular customer, where the staff readily recognize and value their patronage. Regular customers are afforded special treatment which creates a good impression when dining with Korean guests.

Entertaining business friends is a chance to strengthen rapport and impress. Choosing a restaurant that will make everyone comfortable is important. It is difficult to see the "real" person at formal dinner functions so Koreans often prefer informal dinners for business. A willingness to dine Korean style always makes a good impression. Foreigners not yet comfortable with that, might consider a place that offers both Korean and Western dishes. If Korean guests enjoy Western food, consider an exclusive Western style restaurant but expect to dine Korean at some future meeting and prepare accordingly. Korea is loaded with fine restaurants that feature Western style food. The best prepared Western food is usually found at almost any deluxe tourist hotel. International hotel chains like Hyatt, Hilton, etc., have various specialty restaurants that offer everything from simple meals to expensive gourmet dinners.

Most major hotels also feature a buffet restaurant offering a wide variety of foreign and Korean dishes. Expect to pay $25.00 or more per person for lunch, slightly higher for dinner. The food is outstanding and the atmosphere is great for business entertainment. Some suggested buffet restaurants include; the DLI Building, Intercontinental Hotel, and Hilton Hotel to name a few. A reservation is not normally required but it always pays to call ahead during peak periods.

Other fine foreign restaurants are scattered all over Korea especially in large cities. In Seoul, a collection of these establishments are located in the Kangnam area, just south of the Han River. Chinese, Japanese, French, American and a variety of other foreign restaurants are there. Again, the prices are a little higher but the food and service are great.

Dining with important guests is sometimes more comfortable in a private setting. Such dining is common and most fine restaurants offer private rooms as an option. Individual rooms are normally well decorated, comfortable and offer more attentive service. Customers may pay a bit more but the privacy and prestige can be a worthwhile advantage.

When businessmen are not entertaining and would like to eat an inexpensive Western meal without a fancy atmosphere,they could visit  any of the hundreds of common restaurants that serve Western meals. These establishments display a distinctive sign in front advertising that they are designated by the government to serve Western food. This sign was designed to help tourists locate such restaurants more easily,so look for the sign while walking about the city. The prices are more reasonable than hotel restaurants and the food is tasty but don't expect it to be exactly like back home.

Sometimes while on the run, trying to meet a busy schedule, a quick hamburger or other fast food may be in order. All the famous fast food chains are represented in Korea, including McDonald's, Burger King, KFC, Wendy's, Hardee's, Arby's and the most famous American Pizza chains. They are scattered throughout Seoul with clusters in Itaewon, Chongno, Kangnam and other strategic locations.

Hopefully, even the most finicky Westerners will, at least, sample some Korean food during their stay. Korean dishes are quite delicious and nutritious, heavy on vegetables and generally low in fat. There are hundreds of

How to Use Chopsticks

1. Put two sticks between fingers and arrange them on the table.

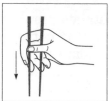

2. Hold sticks on the index finger and middle finger in parallel, and push them with thumb.

3. According to the size of food or thiings, control sticks with index finger and middle finger.

4. Lift food by the power of index finger and middle finger.

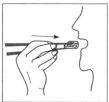

varieties–too many to try and describe here, but experimentation is encouraged. The Korean national dish is *Kimchi*. It is made from cabbage, and is loaded with red pepper and garlic. It is quite tasty, although relatively spicy hot. Those who like spicy dishes normally enjoy *Kimchi*. It is served as a side dish with almost every meal so there are plenty of opportunities to sample it. There are scores of different *Kimchi* dishes and even a *Kimchi* museum where visitors can see how it's prepared and sample different varieties. Some other delicacies include *Pulgogi* (cooked marinated beef) and *Kalbi* (broiled ribs) in either beef or pork. These are two favorites among foreigners but remember meat is a little more expensive here so the cost, for eating portions of beef like back home, may add up quickly. Other common dishes everyone becomes acquainted with include *Yaki Mandu* (similar to egg rolls), *Kimbap* (rice and vegetables rolled in seaweed), *Naeng Myon* (cold soup and noodles) and *Pibimbap* (vegetables and rice) usually served in a hot stone or ceramic bowl and topped with an egg. These dishes are more homestyle so don't try to order them in expensive restaurants, it would be the equivalent of dining at the Ritz and ordering hot dogs. Don't be afraid to sample because Korean food is much more than *Kimchi* and rice. There are hundreds of dishes which include plenty of fish, beef, pork, many kinds of stews, and soups, prepared in a variety of ways mostly unfamiliar to the West.

Traditional Korean restaurants are everywhere, of course, and they also range from the "mom and pop" places to the extravagant. In this case, it may be wise to work backwards, starting with the larger Korean restaurants that cater to foreigners, and work down to the smaller, more authentic places, after acquiring greater familiarity with the local food. It also helps to recruit a friend as a guide. At night, little tents begin popping up all over town serving food and drinks. These individual restaurants are called *Pojang Macha's*. These are the places to eat for foreigners who want to go native. The food is great and the price is very low. The cuisine is likely much different than foreigners are used to so it may be better to ask a friend for suggested dishes that suit individual tastes before an actual visit. It can be interesting and fun to eat in this homey atmosphere alongside the locals. At first glance *Pojang Macha's* may seem less than sanitary but remember they are makeshift places functioning much like an outdoor barbecue. There is little to worry about especially if the food is cooked in hot oil or fried to order.

The key to enjoying meals in Korea is to generally decide what kind of food and what price range is acceptable and then search for that type of restaurant. Be flexible and make time to try the local dishes. Foreigners who take this approach will likely be surprised at how much more enjoyable their Korean experience will become.

Unique Customs

One custom that may catch Westerners off-guard is the way Koreans serve their meals. While Westerners may be accustomed to eating by courses, Koreans tend to serve the entire meal at once with various side dishes to choose from. No one is expected to consume it all since there is usually too much for everyone to finish anyway. It does provide a perfect opportunity to sample new foods however. Dishes are usually communal so guests can select, a little at a time, from several different dishes as they like. As smaller dishes are emptied refills quickly appear. Practice eating with chopsticks, it's fun and more convenient for Korean style dining, but don't be afraid to request a fork, in a restaurant, if chopsticks are completely unmanageable.

Rice is a staple and is served with almost every meal. Koreans usually do not pour soy sauce on their rice but it is not offensive to do so. With some meals rice may not be served until after the main course is through. If rice is desired, with the main course, it may be best to ask. Also, most Korean restaurants still serve their meals on low tables requiring customers to sit on the floor. This can be difficult for some foreigners who can't easily sit "Indian style", but don't worry, modern restaurants also have regular tables too. A few, like the Kum Soo Jung Restaurant at the Ambassador Hotel, and the Sura at the Seoul Hilton even offer low tables with space in the floor underneath for foreigners to let their legs hang comfortably. Korean breakfasts are not the bacon and eggs many Westerners may be used to, but consist of soups and rice etc., similar to other Korean meals. Deserts may also be a little different than expected. Korean restaurants don't normally have a dessert menu as sweets are not usually eaten after a meal. A small portion of fresh fruit is generally served, in place of dessert, adding just a touch of nature's sweetener to a meal. Heavy cakes and pies are not normally available in traditional Korean style restaurants, but ice cream is sometimes offered.

Also don't be surprised if a guest brings a friend to a business dinner without asking. It is not impolite, so be prepared and flexible. It may be advantageous for extra's to join in as they become potential future contacts. If for whatever reason a foreign businessman specifically wants to meet only a certain person or two, he should make that point clear beforehand, using tact and subtlety.

Dinner Conversation

Dinner is a social time not really intended to discuss business. Spend this time talking about general topics of common interest, such as sports, hobbies, travel etc. Remember, however, that Koreans spend more time enjoying the meal rather than carrying on intense discussions. Serious conversation is reserved more for later in the evening during afterdinner drinking sessions. Enjoy the meal and intersperse light superficial conversation. Avoid controversial topics which could spoil the mood such as, politics, religion, etc. Don't fear long periods of silence. Western culture prescribes that if conversation is not lively it may be a sign of boredom. Not so in Korea. Long periods of silence allow for contemplation and are not cause for concern. Silence is actually valued in some contexts and, in Korea, good feelings need not be linked by dialogue. Also, unless all participants are completely fluent in English there will be times when Korean members may talk to each other in Korean and not bother to translate. A Westerner may feel left out of the conversation temporarily but shouldn't become annoyed, the host will ensure everyone is included to keep the mood harmonious. Just remember, the rule is everything in moderation. If there is complete silence the entire evening it may actually be a sign of boredom. If the hosts speak to each other throughout and the Westerner is never included, there may be a slight problem. The point is be flexible and don't be disturbed or feel slighted when encountering some of these situations. Work to keep spirits high and friendly. When two different cultures meet both sides must make some allowances.

DRINKING

After hours rendezvous are a common and necessary occurrence in Korea. As explained before,these meetings are essential to developing the sense of trust necessary for forging the proper relationship conducive to business. In America, going out for drinks normally carries no obligation to become drunk. More often participants are expected to hold their liquor well and certainly not become obnoxiously intoxicated. In Korea, drinking until extreme intoxication is almost expected. It is essential for bonding with other Korean men. A Westerner who is not a drinker must develop some other method to bond with Koreans but it will be difficult to substitute. Drinking and singing together are time tested traditions for developing strong relationships. They provide access to the real person beyond one's official face. The customs associated with this experience may seem a bit awkward and uncomfortable at first. A foreigner can capitalize on the whole experience by preparing to impress his hosts with his knowledge and understanding of their customs.

Room Salon

This unique style of entertainment offers a private room for members to unwind away from the scrutiny of others. A room salon usually consists of a number of private rooms available for multiple parties by different customers. The rooms are comfortably furnished with a central table surrounded by sofa style seating. A group, usually three to six members (but can include as many as an expense account can afford), reserve a private room within the room salon for their evening entertainment. Members enjoy drinking and *anju* (Korean side dishes) while getting to know each other. But eating and drinking are not the main reasons for visiting a room salon. Female company is the main attraction. Hostesses are expected to join the party, usually one or more per customer. Contrary to popular belief, modern hostesses at room salons provide and enhance entertainment by pouring drinks, conversing, laughing at jokes, dancing, singing, and generally keeping spirits high. They are not expected to engage in any sexual behavior on the premises although some hostesses may agree to meet customers after work for a date,etc., depending entirely on the individual customer and hostess.

Sometime after first arriving, various women are brought to the table to serve as partners. If a particular partner is not pleasing, politely and discreetly inform the host who will arrange to switch to another girl from another room. Don't feel embarrassed by it, the hostesses are used to it and a customer should feel comfortable with a partner to ensure the most pleasant evening. Don't abuse this system however; if a guest is too picky, the host may feel he is not providing a good time which may sour the mood. Bottom line, change once maybe twice, if the hostess just doesn't match, but otherwise remain flexible and have a good time with the partner provided. Remember, these hostesses will receive a hefty tip for their services, usually starting at around 50,000 won. The host usually tips all the hostesses, at the conclusion of the party, so when planning to host such a gathering be prepared for this cost.

Most room salons expect customers to drink hard liquor, mainly Scotch whiskey. Along with the drinks, *anju*, or side dishes, are usually ordered. A variety of *anju* is available including, fresh fruit, fish, nuts, etc., some obviously more expensive than others. Again, the host will usually order all this and pay at the end. When the liquor arrives, the basic rule is no one pours his own drink. A foreign guest should attempt to pour for the host, or others who outrank him, and they will be quick to pour for the guest. When pouring, always use two hands or one outstretched hand with the other touching the arm symbolizing two hands. Do not pour with the left hand as it is impolite. When receiving a drink, hold the glass with two hands. Whiskey is usually poured into shot glasses. After finishing a glass it is customary to pass it to another, usually the host first, then pour a drink for that person. Others will likely be passing glasses also and spirits can flow quickly. A Western guest who is not a heavy drinker should empty his glass slowly, a good host will get the message and not push a guest to drink too much. A good hostess can also be of assistance in this regard, helping to water down or empty the glass to keep the mood of the party happy and prevent the guest from looking or feeling awkward. Be cautious about offering female partners drinks. It is polite to do so occasionally but remember, liquor is expensive and the host will probably appreciate using it wisely amongst guests. Let him offer drinks to the hostesses as he desires.

Sometime during the evening, the host may order a private band to play for the group. The band is usually one person, with an electronic music system on wheels. It is not there to entertain the group, but actually to accompany members of the party who wish to sing. Koreans love to sing, especially while drinking, and foreigners will make a good impression if they take a turn. No need to worry too much about ability, Koreans realize everyone may not be talented singers but it's the shared experience that matters. The band usually has a few song books with both Korean and American favorites. It should be relatively easy to find one to sing. If a guest is extra shy his partner may help him through the tune. A smart businessman prepares for this occasion by practicing at least one song for such a party but better to prepare two in case an encore is demanded. Learning a Korean song will make an even better impression. Of course the band is also an added expense incurred by the host so foreigners must consider this when planning such a party themselves. If after acquiring some experience, a Westerner decides to host an evening at a room salon, it's wise to consult a

Korean friend to help arrange the appropriate entertainment at the right place for the best results. Room salons come in all varieties ranging from the simple and slightly expensive to the extravagant and extremely costly. A party of four can easily finish four or more Korean size bottles in an evening. Regular customers may establish a tab and a bottle in the customer's name. Whiskey is expensive in room salons so customers may save the unfinished portion of a particular bottle, at the establishment, for the next visit. Room salons generally accept most major credit cards.

Karaoke

Similar to room salons in some respects, karaoke has also become popular in recent years. Most offer the same drinking and eating arrangements as room salons. However, karaoke focuses around one activity, singing. The idea was adapted from Japan where it has been popular somewhat longer. In Korea, karaoke bars, are mainly small with tables partitioned for limited privacy. Most feature a main stage with either a band or a laser disc video system which provides the music to accompany the singer. As the music is playing, the lyrics appear at the bottom of the screen to help guests sing along. Karaoke's often have individual rooms for small groups to sing more privately. Unlike room salons, it is more acceptable to bring a date but hostesses may also be available as partners, again for a large tip. Prices in karaoke bars are similar to those in room salons so a foreigner must be prepared if he is the host. Like room salons, karaokes come in various configurations and designs, so explore.

Noraebang

A modern sensation in Korea, these singing rooms are low budget practice facilities for the die-hard singing enthusiast. They have sprouted seemingly on every street corner and are used by all types of citizens to practice their favorite tunes or sing away some daily stress. Each individual room is small, usually tightly seating about six persons. Rooms are spartan with a basic table, padded chairs and a laser disk player. Most *noraebang's* require payment by the hour, usually about 12-15,000 won. Liquor is prohibited but customers may purchase soft drinks and snacks. It's a great place to practice some tunes before meeting with business contacts where singing will likely be required. These establishments have become so popular that some businesses have installed them in the work place for their employees. It really is a lot of fun and the practice ultimately improves singing ability. Foreigners who sing with their Korean friends can certainly strengthen their business relationships.

Nightclubs & Cabarets

Attracting a slightly older clientele, these establishments usually feature a stage variety show and plenty of singing and live music. A large dance floor affords the opportunity for customers to kick up their heels if they like and it's acceptable to bring a date or request a hostess as a partner if preferred. Like most other entertainment establishments customers are expected to purchase some liquor and *anju* and there is usually a minimum table charge. If the company of a hostess is preferred, a fee similar to that at room salons is required. Most major hotels contain a nightclub but the music and atmospheres differ so shop around for one that suits a particular taste. Cabarets are peppered throughout the city and usually provide a mixture of ballroom dance music and some disco dance numbers.

Hofs

German style beer halls are quite popular in larger

cities. They feature a casual atmosphere to drink and talk with friends. Various *anju* plates are available including sausages, potatoes, etc., to enjoy with the drinks. Koreans normally drink beer from a glass and remember no one pours their own. The American custom of drinking from the bottle is impolite probably because it precludes pouring drinks for each other. When hosting friends, a hof can be a nice place to go after dinner or as an early first stop before proceeding to more serious drinking at a room salon or karaoke.

Western Style Lounges

A few Western style lounges are popular for foreigners and are mainly located at major hotel chains. In Seoul, JJ Mahoney's at the Hyatt hotel offers a Jazz bar, with live band, on one side and a disco on the other. The Hyatt also offers a more quiet piano bar (Regency Bar) one floor below the lobby. O'Kims at the Westin Chosun Hotel is an Irish sports bar with live music on most nights. Bobby London, at the Lotte Hotel, is an English pub with music and a casual atmosphere. This style night spot may be a welcome change of pace for Koreans on occasion. Itaewon has many Western style bars that are very casual, and may be more appealing to foreigners but are not normally well suited for entertaining Korean business contacts. There are some Korean clubs in Itaewon, however, that are more suitable for business entertainment.

SAUNAS

One of the great relaxing moments in Korea comes from a visit to the sauna. More than just a bath, these facilities are usually luxurious and come in a variety of decor. Upon entering, customers are provided a locker for safe storage of clothing only. Any valuables would be safer in the separate locked deposit box available at the entrance counter. After undressing customers normally proceed from the locker to the sauna, nude, and enter a shower area to rinse off in preparation for the actual sauna. Facilities vary but better saunas include a choice of dry saunas, steam rooms, herbal rooms, and others. Following some time in any or all of the sauna rooms, it's time to try a relaxing bath in three separate pools; one very hot, one medium and one icy cold. From there another wash area is provided for brushing teeth, shaving,etc. Guests exit the sauna area to a grooming room to dry off, style their hair,etc. Finer saunas employ a barber to assist customers but his services are not always free. Massages are often available, normally in separate but attached rooms,and the fee is extra. Another option is to just relax, put on a robe (provided) and read the paper or lounge in the TV room. Some facilities even contain a small restaurant to enjoy light meals and drinks. Customers may stay as long as they like. The price for all this is reasonable, 8-12,000 won. It's typical to spend about 1 1/2 hours, after work, usually before going out in the evening.

PAYING THE CHECK
— A LITTLE DIFFERENT THAN YOU'RE USED TO

Westerners are often surprised the first few times they see several Koreans fighting to pay the check. Korea is not the place for "going dutch". Such behavior is considered petty and impolite. Normally the host or person who invites pays the bill. Even among Westerners who know this custom there is sometimes a temptation to break even by counting who paid last time. The phrase "I'll pay this time you paid last time" is also not recommended. Don't keep tabs on how many times who bought who lunch. The host should always expect to pay. If the foreigner is the host remember, at the end of the meal other guests may try to pay as a polite gesture, but don't let them. Hence the struggle at the cash register. For important engagements, arrange to take care of the bill in advance or after the guests have left so no check appears at the end of the meal. This will add a nice touch and indicate the foreigner is an important regular customer at that establishment.

TIPPING — WHAT IS APPROPRIATE WHEN?

Rendering the proper tip can be tricky in a foreign land. Generally tipping is not a custom of Korea and is not required in restaurants or coffee shops. There are exceptions however. A standard gratuity is added in major hotels and international establishments. As previously explained, tipping is mandatory for hostesses in room salons and similar entertainment places. Tipping is expected for those providing special services, like the movers who set up the apartment, or the valet who parks the car,etc. Taxi drivers are not tipped however, neither are waitresses so don't leave a tip on the table after a meal. Large tips are usually expected in barber shops especially if a customer receives extra services. Foreigners should learn what is appropriate,as a well placed tip will impress Korean business contacts and likely yield special service the next time they return.

OTHER ENTERTAINMENT

To further strengthen relationships after sharing experiences at the establishments mentioned above, I suggest spending time together in a different way. Consider taking in a show, sporting event, or tourist attraction together.

Home or Office

Although little entertaining is actually done in either place, there will certainly be occasion for Korean acquaintances to stop by the foreigner's office for meetings or courtesy calls. In all cases it is appropriate to serve guests some refreshments without asking. Most appropriate is juice, tea, or coffee. Soft drinks are not recommended unless requested. The office should have a small area to sit comfortably and talk away from the desk. Usually a few chairs, sofa and coffee table will do. If a certain person rarely visits, take photos and prepare a personalized memento to present the guest. Most Korean homes are small and not conducive to entertaining Western Style but if treated to a visit to someone's home consider it special. Take a small gift such as fruit or baked goods for the hosts.

Sports

Playing sports together or attending spectator sporting events are great ways to share experiences. Golf is popular, among businessmen in Korea and local courses are very scenic, well groomed and relatively expensive. Before golfing with Korean clients or friends try to learn a few golf terms in Korean to use on the course. A lot of golf terminology is derived from the English so common phrases such as "nice par" or "nice putt," will be understood by Korean partners, although they may be pronounced with an accent. However, expressing a few phrases in Korean will impress Korean partners and be very much appreciated (see chapter 9 for a few examples). Other terms are expressed in English but were formed in a way Westerners may not be familiar with; for example, "out course" meaning the front nine holes and "in course" meaning, the back nine holes of the course. It makes sense, it's just different. Another set includes "long hole" meaning a par five, "middle hole" meaning a par four, and "short hole" meaning a par three. That famous "gimme" putt is called "give" (pronounced in two syllables like "gee bu") in Korean.

Driving ranges are another golf option for spending time together and are less time consuming and less costly. Quality ranges include attached saunas and restaurants so it's easy to spend several hours relaxing there together. Tennis is a popular sport conducive for relationship-building and the many courts in the Seoul area are always crowded with enthusiasts. With winter begins the ski season and, whether a beginner or expert, there are slopes to match everyone's ability. Korean ski resorts are ultra modern and fun for the whole family. International sporting events are frequently held in Korea so it's possible to see a boxing, swimming, gymnastics, or some other sports contest. Also, Korea has a professional baseball league and attending a game with a friend can be fun.

Tourism

Koreans are proud of their country and there is much to see and do. Westerners who show an interest in the history and culture will usually have Korean friends anxious to show them around. Take advantage of the opportunity. Whether the interest is in mountains, beaches, museums, temples, palaces, resorts or a variety of other attractions, Korea has it all. Use these locations as a way to spend quality time with Korean business contacts.

GIFT GIVING — THE THOUGHT COUNTS A LOT

Deciding on the right gift for the appropriate occasion can be frustrating in a foreign country. Certain occasions require a gift and others present opportunities to win extra favor by providing an unexpected but appropriate present. Remember, some gifts may create certain obligations but the best ones carry no perception of obligation, while leaving the receiver in high spirits wanting to repay without being so obliged. When visiting someone's home a small gift is always appropriate. Fruit or baked goods are popular choices. Gifts for the family, especially children, are in good taste. In the case of weddings or funerals, money is most appropriate and a card is not necessary. Cash, in all circumstances, is given in white envelopes. When visiting a friend in the hospital, fruit is most often given. Proper gifts for Korean business friends are essential. Imported items or articles from a foreigner's hometown are always welcome. Keeping a stock of small mementos relating to the company, such as quality pen sets, pins, leather binders, decorative paperweights and other attractive items can be useful when Koreans visit your office. Unexpectedly presenting something to remember their visit will be appreciated and win a Westerner favor. Also, if any photos are taken, be sure to present them courtesy copies. Whatever is given, make sure it is high quality so it creates a positive long-lasting impression. Make sure to present higher level counterparts with more prestigious items commensurate with their position. Keep track of what is given to whom. It is embarrassing to make a presentation only to discover that person was given the same gift on a previous visit. Such a mistake definitely signals insincerity and could harm a relationship. Don't be afraid to ask for advice if not sure of the most appropriate gift for a special occasion. Gift giving can be an excellent opportunity to show sincerity and concern for close Korean friends and a knowledge of Korean customs. Use each opportunity wisely and plan it well to maximize the benefit.

6

LIVING IN MODERN KOREA

HOUSING

Apartments - What to Expect

One look around the capital and it's easy to see the forest of modern apartment buildings throughout the city. Most high-rise apartment buildings are very modern but there are a few differences to expect while searching for a place to live.

First, expect smaller apartments than most Westerners are accustomed to, large Western style apartments are significantly more expensive. However, modern Korean apartments are comfortable and easy to adjust to with a little preparation. Remember some apartments are older than others and generally, the newer the apartment, the more Western conveniences are likely to be included. For example, most Korean apartments do not have built-in closets. Koreans normally purchase beautiful, sometimes ornate, portable closets for their homes. However, newer apartments are including closets in their floor plans more often. Foreigners are often surprised to learn that their large Western furniture does not fit well in smaller Korean apartments, so it's wise to plan ahead.

Generally, kitchens are smaller and offer less cabinet space than American kitchens. They are often absent some luxury appliances such as dishwashers or full size ranges.

The bathroom may also look a little different. Western style toilets are standard but many Korean homes feature "wet baths" which are tiled and have no shower curtain so the bathroom may become soaked during a shower. That's why many home bathrooms have rubber slippers for use by guests when they enter, because the floor may be somewhat wet and preclude entry in stocking feet.

Most apartment buildings have security guards at the entry to the first floor. This man is important and tenants should treat him well. The security guard is the eyes and ears of the complex. He can not only watch the apartment but can keep a close eye on the vehicles in the parking lot if so inclined. Little acts of kindness to the guard will make him inclined to care for you a little more diligently. When living in an apartment all the utilities, except telephone, are likely to be included in one itemized monthly bill. Electricity can be expensive if major appliances such as an air conditioner are used.

Some older apartments and office buildings may not have a fourth floor so labeled because of the old superstition of four as an unlucky number. It originates from the fact that the Chinese character for the number four is pronounced the same as the character for death. It is considered unlucky, much like the number thirteen in the West. The superstition appears to be dying out but some people still prefer not to live on the fourth floor.

Pyong - Unique Measuring System

While Westerners may be accustomed to measuring apartment space in square feet or square meters, *pyong* is the unit of measurement of living space in Korea. It pays to become familiar with this measurement if foreigners plan to rent or buy office space, or living quarters, in Korea. One *pyong* is roughly equivalent to six square feet or .54 square meters. It was derived from an old Koguryo system of measuring based on "*chok*" which was a primitive ruler. Five *chok*, roughly the equivalent of a full step, was called a "*po*". Twentyfive square *chok* was called a *pyong*. This system was later adopted by the Japanese who changed the measurement slightly for their own use. At any rate, it has remained popular today and is the standard in Korea.

When apartment space is calculated foreigners should carefully compare the spaces of different apartments. Some size quotations may include nonliving spaces such as small balconies or even outside halls. It pays to ask specifically what space is included in a particular calculation to prevent misunderstanding the actual size. Some commercial properties may provide comparative information of space in Western figures but foreigners may have to ask to obtain it.

Rent System - Uniquely Korean

Unlike renting in America, where apartment owners require a monthly rent with a deposit of first and last months rent in advance, the Korean system is quite different. In fact, it is not really a rent system at all. It is called "*Chonsay*" and amounts to renter's depositing a large sum of money with the landlord and then living rent-free for a period, usually a year, then receiving the lump sum back upon moving. The landlord essentially profits from the interest derived from investing that large sum. This can be a convenient way to pay for housing except that foreigners are often not prepared to deposit such large sums when they arrive in Korea. The sum can range from $60,000 and up.

Some landlords will negotiate "*Wolsay*", which is a monthly rate, but they will usually still require a large security deposit, around 4-8 million won depending on the total value of the apartment. Needless to say, foreigners should have a lease or contract before depositing any large sums of money with a landlord.

Hotels - There is a Difference

When travelling in any foreign country accommodations become a critical factor in a successful trip. Depending on a foreigner's taste and budget Korea offers a wide variety of lodging to fit any travel plans. There are several ways to classify hotel accommodations in Korea but I will focus on describing three basic styles: deluxe hotels, tourist hotels, and *yogwans.*

Korea is a modern country and Seoul, the capital, has some of the finest facilities in the world. So if luxury is the specific desire there are many fine hotels to choose from beginning with the international chains such as Hilton, Hyatt, Ramada, to locally run deluxe hotels such as Lotte and Shilla and many others. Hotels in this class offer ultra-modern facilities including various restaurants, saunas, bars, meeting rooms, business centers, and a host of other conveniences all in an atmosphere of splendor. These hotels are most often conveniently located near major business and shopping areas and provide the most efficient and attentive service available. Of course, expect to pay more for such comfort but prices vary and be sure to check for discounts. Other areas in Korea like Pusan, Chejudo, etc., also have this level of accommodations available. They cater to business needs and are excellent meeting places.

If a Western style hotel without expensive frills is preferred then a tourist hotel may be a good choice. In Seoul, this may include a variety of slightly lower class facilities ranging from the Holiday Inn, Hamilton, Tower, etc., down to the Yongdong, New Naija, or Astoria class. In most areas, outside of Seoul, tourist hotels will often be the highest class of lodging available and will usually range from $60.00 and up. These hotels offer a Western style room, private bath, and some conveniences such as limited restaurants and a lower profile atmosphere.

One of the best kept lodging secrets are Korean *yogwans.* These mini-hotels were originally Korean style with mats or cushions on the floor for sleeping and little or no furniture in very cramped rooms. Modern *yogwans* however, have transformed into wonderful, inexpensive lodging, especially for those who spend their vacations away from their hotel rooms and do not require an abundance of conveniences. Most *yogwans* offer a choice of Western or Korean style rooms, all neat and clean with private baths. Styles and decor vary so don't be afraid to look around. These small but comfortable facilities provide excellent lodging while allowing customers to keep more of their hard earned money to spend elsewhere.

If an extended stay is planned, travelers may want to mix and match, staying in some *yogwans* and some deluxe or tourist hotels. Whatever a foreigner's needs, be it strictly business, pleasure or budget consciousness, Korea has the lodging to match.

Addresses - An Unfamiliar Method

As mentioned in chapter 3, the address system is, in a way, opposite to the West. Besides the fact that they are written from the largest unit to the smallest (city first, house number last), addresses can be very difficult to understand and locate. Westerners are used to working with a grid system so any address can be pinpointed by locating the nearest two cross streets. Western addresses are numbered along a street so that once the proper street is found it can be followed to the exact address. Not so in Korea. First of all, streets were rarely named until very recently. Secondly, addresses are determined within the boundaries of a certain area, called a *Dong* in Korean. Within this area, roughly the size of a few square blocks, individual buildings are numbered. In a large city like Seoul, there are hundreds of *dongs* and no way to know which one is where without memorizing them or referring to a map. This can present some frustration if a foreigner tries to locate an address on his own. In a large city, landmarks such as tall buildings can help with some directions from a friend, but otherwise it can be difficult to locate independently. In more modern apartment complexes, where scores of families live in one building, each building may be designated a *dong*, which makes it easier to locate. Whatever the case, the *dong* is an important administrative unit in the city. It may be better compared to a precinct, in Western terms. There are about 523 of these precincts in Seoul. Within a city, the next higher administrative unit is the *Gu*, which some compare to a ward. Seoul is presently divided into 22 *gu's*. In the country, areas are divided into *Gun* (pronounced more like goon) and *Myon*. *Gun's* are similar to counties and *myon* could be compared to a township. There are smaller administrative units both in the city and country but the ones mentioned here are probably the most important.

SHOPPING

Shopping in Korea is still very exciting. Korea has long had a reputation for marvelous bargains. Remember however, prices fluctuate everywhere and Korea is no exception. For more than a decade, this country has sustained tremendous modernization and growth which included a certain amount of corresponding inflation. In other words, the days of the $3.00 tennis shoes and such are gone. Many people still arrive with dated expectations of prices and mumble how expensive Korea has become. Prices are certainly higher but bargains still abound. The foreigner who does his homework, and compares current prices, will have a much more pleasurable shopping experience and will better appreciate the discounts he receives.

A few cultural tips may also help find the best values. First, remember that wherever a person shops in Korea, arriving early in the morning makes them a special status customer. The first customer, in almost any shop, is customarily an important sale. Koreans believe the initial sale will basically determine the tempo of the day's activities. In other words, if the first customer leaves without buying anything then business will likely be slow that day. Conversely, a large first sale is a sign of good luck. Shoppers who visit a store early may be able to bargain for the best price of the day. But please go prepared to buy and no window shopping early in the morning. If a customer haggles and doesn't buy something it will ruin the shop owner's day and may arouse his anger. Plan ahead. If shoppers know what they want they can likely get a good deal that will please both them and the shop owner. One word of caution, don't try to blackmail the owner with this custom. Stay good natured and be firm without being unreasonable.

Know your shopping area. Every shop is not a discount store. Large department stores offer imported items at some very steep prices. As anywhere in the world if customers want the best quality they must pay a little more. In other words, if a customer wants an imitation Rolex watch in Itaewon, fine, but remember, it is imitation and is not close to the quality of the real ones sold in duty free shops for thousands of dollars.

Haggling for prices is fun and part of the charm of shopping in Korea. Some tourists have remarked "haggling is easy, just offer half of whatever price the salesman quotes and bargain from there. " Negotiating a real bargain is not that simple. Remember, each product has a different markup. While customers may bargain some clothes down 50% off the original asking price, that kind of discount may not be possible when buying luggage or other goods. If customers insist on trying to push an owner below a price he can afford both will be frustrated. Be smart about quality. When buying suits for example, there are a variety of different grades of fabric with very different prices, and if shoppers are not sure what they're buying they could be taken.

Again, shoppers who do their homework and know a good price when they hear it will sincerely strengthen their negotiating power and ultimate satisfaction. The bottom line is know the product, spend time comparing quality and prices and have fun exploring the thousands of shops and outlets offering terrific values just waiting for eager shoppers.

CRIME

Foreigners should be happy to learn Korea has a relatively low crime rate, far lower than most Western countries. That does not mean Korea is crime free. There are murders, rapes, thefts, burglaries, swindlers and pickpockets and other criminals, similar to other countries, just far fewer of them. Korea even has a growing drug problem but again it is relatively small by American comparison. Violent crimes are rare, especially against foreigners, and 1990's crimes like carjackings are unheard of. Even car thefts are almost non-existent. The crime most likely to affect foreigners will be petty theft and, depending where a foreigner lives, housebreaking. Even burglars have a code of conduct in Korea. Most will not enter a house where people are sleeping and if they accidentally choose a home that's occupied a simple cough will often send them on their way.

Korean Police handle crime much differently, in many ways, from police in America. Don't be surprised if police refuse to get involved in a domestic disturbance or even a fist fight in the street. In America, police would usually swoop down quickly and subdue the participants whisking them off to the police station to sort out the altercation. Korean police are more likely to let the individuals sort it out. Police may even stand by and observe, allowing friends or others to break up such a fight. A general rule might be, if it can be resolved by those involved let it be so. America is in general a more legalistic society and Americans often choose litigation for conflict resolution. Koreans try to resolve conflict themselves, maybe including a third party as arbitrator, if possible. Traffic accidents are an appropriate example. Minor traffic accidents are usually discussed among those involved and a resolution reached at the scene. Sometimes money is even exchanged before both parties depart. Only if they cannot agree, or if serious injury is involved, will they resort to police and insurance companies for assistance.

WEIGHT AND MEASURES

It is sometimes a bit of a shock for some foreigners who are accustomed to measuring distances in miles, buying gasoline by the gallon, and judging temperature by degrees Fahrenheit, to discover that Korea is metric. Although they should not be surprised, foreigners often tend to overlook this little detail until faced with a task of deciphering their new enviroment.

This may not seem important but it pays to know your height and weight, for example, using a system you can compare with your Korean friends. These few charts will help make the conversions a little less intimidating.

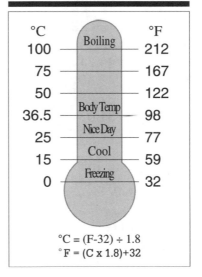

TEMPERATURE

°C		°F
100	Boiling	212
75		167
50		122
36.5	Body Temp	98
25	Nice Day	77
15	Cool	59
0	Freezing	32

$$°C = (F-32) ÷ 1.8$$
$$°F = (C \times 1.8)+32$$

HEIGHT / LENGTH

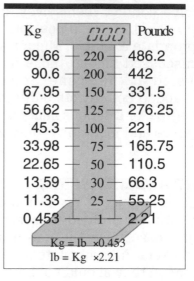

Cm		Inch
457.2	180	70.92
406.4	160	63.04
254	100	39.4
228.6	90	35.46
203.2	80	31.52
127	50	19.7
101.6	40	15.76
76.2	30	11.82
38.1	15	5.91
2.54	1	0.394

$$Cm = Inch \times 2.54$$
$$Inch = Cm \times 0.394$$

WEIGHT

Kg		Pounds
99.66	220	486.2
90.6	200	442
67.95	150	331.5
56.62	125	276.25
45.3	100	221
33.98	75	165.75
22.65	50	110.5
13.59	30	66.3
11.33	25	55.25
0.453	1	2.21

$$Kg = lb \times 0.453$$
$$lb = Kg \times 2.21$$

DISTANCE

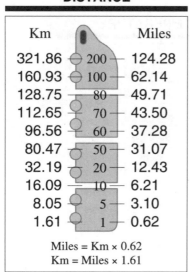

Km		Miles
321.86	200	124.28
160.93	100	62.14
128.75	80	49.71
112.65	70	43.50
96.56	60	37.28
80.47	50	31.07
32.19	20	12.43
16.09	10	6.21
8.05	5	3.10
1.61	1	0.62

$$Miles = Km \times 0.62$$
$$Km = Miles \times 1.61$$

7

TRANSPORTATION

DRIVING IN KOREA

For many visitors, getting behind the wheel of a car in Korea is a frustrating, even frightening, experience. Especially in Seoul, traffic is often thick, the pace is quick, and traffic rules seem to be ignored. Cars seem to weave in and out without regard to traffic lines or safety, and when you try to merge no one seems to give in. Drivers often turn three lanes into six, squeezing in between vehicles wherever there is the smallest space. Taxis and buses appear the worst offenders, stopping quickly to pick up passengers at any spot along the street, failing to pull completely out of traffic causing disruption and sometimes near accidents. Buses merge seemingly at will using their mammoth size to force common motorists out of their way or risk injury. Drivers in general, seem to merge quickly, without signal, cutting off other motorists without remorse, horns blaring to clear a path. Pedestrians walk in the street seemingly without regard for their own safety, sometimes venturing out one or two lanes to hail a taxi or be the first in line for the bus. And of course, everyone has seen the pedestrians who cross eight lanes of traffic, before looking, with one hand out to stop traffic, oblivious to the thousands of pounds of speeding steel capable of smashing them into the next world. Bicycles and motorcycles are often used as trucks carrying heavy loads stacked high in the air dangerously susceptible to sudden wind gusts and dependent on the balancing skills of their drivers. Trucks too are often loaded far beyond safe limits causing accidents and breakdowns which result in injury or snarl traffic even further. Korea's fatality rate from accidents was the highest in the world at the end of 1992. This apparent madness on the highways leaves many foreigners shaking their heads or worse, cursing the apparently rude behavior of the natives.

Korea has some major traffic problems to be sure, but much of the frustration foreigners experience may be the result of trying to drive in Korea as they did back home. Despite all the observations and negative reaction of foreigners there is some method to the apparent madness and knowing the customs can make driving here not only safer but more enjoyable and certainly less stressful.

There are two important concepts to remember that can make driving much more pleasant. First, weaving in and out of traffic is a way of life but contrary to popular belief, it is not performed indiscriminately. Almost every driver knows that to move ahead of someone in traffic a driver must position the nose of his vehicle ahead of their's. This will allow the driver the "right of way" so to speak. If one driver is clearly in that position the other driver will let him in. If he is not clearly in that position the other driver may try to reposition himself ahead of the merging driver, forcing him to try and merge ahead of the next car. Try to keep the vehicle moving while merging. Do not stop and try to merge, if the traffic is moving at all, as this causes much more disruption. There is no magic to this method. With a little practice, a skilled driver may easily flow through several lanes of traffic within a short distance. After merging, a polite driver always thanks the driver behind by raising his hand or nodding his head. This acknowledges the courtesy of one driver allowing another to merge in front.

Second, the horn is not routinely used as an expression of anger, which is often the case in the West. It is most often used as a signal to alert another driver when someone is passing or entering a blind spot etc. This is essential in traffic where there is much lane changing. When changing lanes quickly it is sometimes difficult to be seen well by the other driver and an accident could result. Use a short burst of the horn to alert the driver ahead, or to the side, that you are advancing.

Remember, holding up your right hand after merging acknowledges the driver's indiscretion and in a sense, begs pardon for his actions. It is polite to do so and keeps tensions much lower between drivers. It is not however, a license to drive without regard for others. Keep the first two concepts in mind, and use this gesture in conjunction, then observe the difference in getting around. It will likely take much of the pain, or fear, out of driving in Korea.

Police are enforcing traffic regulations more strictly, like making illegal turns, or using a bus lane etc. Where they used to turn a blind eye to violations by foreigners, that trend is reversing, so the old "I'm a foreigner and didn't know" excuse may not work anymore. Another area of increased emphasis involves drunk driving which is no stranger to Western countries either. Police have made a much stronger enforcement effort in this regard and there are plenty of alternate means of transportation when a person has been drinking, so DON'T DRINK AND DRIVE.

TAXIS — WHAT SHOULD I KNOW?

If a Westerner is unfamiliar with his destination, especially in large cities, one of the best means of transportation to ensure arrival at that important appointment on time is the common taxi. Generally, it is fast, inexpensive and safe. However, in the past taxi drivers have developed a less than excellent reputation among visitors, some of it deserved, some of it not. Understanding the system and working within it can greatly affect whether a foreigner has a positive experience. A closer look at how taxis operate may help foreigners feel more comfortable using them.

Basically, there are two types of taxis, standard and deluxe. The standard taxi comes in various colors and models. They comfortably seat three passengers and the trunk should handle basic luggage but is not overly spacious. Don't expect service such as loading bags, although a kind driver may do so. Taxi drivers do not expect a tip, unless of course he provides an extra service or act of courtesy. The driver may not speak English so it's wise to have the destination written in Korean by hotel personnel or a friend.

Deluxe taxis (also called *Mobom taxis* in Korean) are luxury cabs. Distinctive gloss black with a wide gold stripe on the side and a yellow sign on top, these taxis offer a higher level of service and comfort. The drivers are uniformed and courteous. Expect them to open doors when possible and load luggage. Legally, these cabs can only take passengers at special taxi stands, hotels, bus terminals and certain other locations. Of course, this increased service is more expensive.

All taxi fares are calculated on a meter displayed on the front dashboard. The fare is based on the basic minimum plus distance and time. Standard taxis cost 1,000 won for the first two kilometers and 100 won for each additional 279 meters. If you are stuck in traffic and the taxi reduces speed to less than 15km per hour, an additional 100 won will be added every 67 seconds. Deluxe taxis start at 3,000 won for the first 3km and 200 won for each additional 250 meters, and 200 won every 60 seconds when the speed drops below 15km per hour. These fares add up quickly. The usual fare from the airport to downtown is 8-10,000 won in a standard taxi and 23-25,000 won in a deluxe. It could be higher in heavy traffic and fares increase 20% after midnight. Deluxe taxis also provide receipts.

Often, standard taxis like to take on additional passengers that happen to be going the same way. Koreans call this *Hapsung*. With less taxis than people who need them it is convenient for citizens, who can catch a cab more easily, and attractive for taxi drivers who can pick up extra money from the extra fares. It can also benefit foreigners when they need a cab and can't find an empty one. To use this system, a passenger should just call out the destination as a cab goes by and if it is going near there, the driver will let the passenger board. Now the confusing part begins. If a passenger boards this way the local custom is to pay the driver by the meter reading from when the passenger boarded to when he gets off, plus an additional 500 won. For example, if a passenger boards when the meter is at 1,500 won and gets off at 2,700 won, the passenger would pay 1,700 won. Also remember a passenger can never pay less than the basic minimum fare of 1,000 won. For example if a passenger boarded when the meter read 1,500 won and got off 2,200 won he would have to pay at least the basic fare of 1,000 won. Visitors sometimes become confused or feel cheated using this system and complaints often result. For this reason the government discourages *hapsung* rides, especially with foreigners, who are less likely to understand the custom. Deluxe taxis are prohibited from using this method.

Most taxi drivers are not out to take advantage of foreigners but most complaints occur from the airport into town where some unscrupulous drivers have been noted. If a foreigner has a problem with a taxi driver, there are tourist complaint centers, in major cities, to assist. Always remember to obtain the important identifying information about the taxi which is usually displayed on the dashboard. Keep in mind, problems often result from misunderstanding or miscommunication and a little kindness can resolve many such instances.

Armed with this knowledge of the system, and a little flexibility, foreigners will discover taxis really are the quickest and easiest method of getting around.

BUSES — INEXPENSIVE AND EFFICIENT

The most inexpensive means of transportation, next to walking, is the common city bus. Taking a bus in a foreign country can be intimidating, however, with a basic knowledge of the system, and a little daring, a foreigner can turn the bus system into a means of transportation that can save money and can actually be fun.

There are basically three kinds of city buses in Seoul; regular, express and airport buses. At first glance, regular buses can seem the most intimidating. All the destinations are written in Korean, passengers must use exact change, the drivers do not usually speak English and they stop and go so quickly passengers don't seem to have time to ask questions. Actually, these buses do stop and go quickly, as they run very frequently and try to stay on schedule despite traffic delays. This is of definite benefit as passengers are rarely forced to wait long to catch the next one. The destinations are written in Korean, on the sides, but all the buses are numbered with large numerals on all sides in two colors, red and blue. Each number corresponds to a bus route and if a foreigner learns the number of the route he wants he can spot the correct bus easily. The colors also indicate where the bus stops. Foreigners should have a friend or any hotel direct them to the right stop and provide the correct number. Catch the same number bus to return to the original destination. The exact change is 300 won or passengers may purchase bus tokens for a slight discount but at this price it's really not worth the trouble. Expect crowds on most regular buses and passengers may have to stand most of the trip. However, the trips are usually short so it's not much of a problem to ride without a seat. Buses are quick and safe and will certainly provide some insight into how millions of Koreans travel everyday.

Express buses have more seats than regular buses and make fewer stops along the way. They are green and have numbers on the sides like regular city buses.

These buses are twice as expensive but still a bargain. Again, foreigners can ask a friend or hotel personnel to help determine the right number and location for the bus they need. When riding any bus it helps to know when to exit by having it written in Korean. Show it to the driver in advance and he will usually be willing to signal when the bus has reached that destination. Every bus stop has a sign post which lists the numbers of all the buses which stop there. Foreigners may refer to it to be sure they are waiting at the right stop. Airport buses are available from many hotels and major locations in Seoul. They make few stops, are comfortable and cheaper than a taxi. Major hotels can assist in catching this bus at the passenger's time of departure. Certain airlines such as Northwest, Cathay Pacific, Asiana and others have baggage check-in and airport bus service from the Korea City Air Terminal in southern Seoul. Buses departing from this location are direct to Kimpo Airport.

Whether a foreigner is on a tight budget or just wants to try something different, taking the bus can be fun. Taking the bus avoids driving in traffic and both the difficulty and expense of finding parking. The money saved in parking fees alone may make it worthwhile. The system looks ominous at first but once foreigners have done it a few times they are usually surprised how easy it actually is.

SUBWAY — QUICK AND EASY TO USE

The various myths about the subway system in Seoul, may sometimes discourage businessmen from using it. Some think the subway is just for the locals. Others think it's only for those who speak Korean, and still others believe it's too crowded or too complicated for foreigners. Nothing could be further from the truth. The Seoul subway is one of the fastest, most inexpensive, convenient and user-friendly systems of its size in the world.

Four, color coded, subway lines crisscross the city to almost anywhere users need to go. The green line is the longest with forty three stops on both sides of the Han River. It passes some major places of interest such as the Korea World Trade Center, Lotte World, Olympic Sports Complex, six universities and straight through the center of downtown Seoul to City Hall and the central business district. Don't worry much about getting lost because the green line happens to be the only one that is a loop so eventually it always returns to the place it began. The blue line is the next longest and begins south of the Han and traverses the city, north and east, stopping at key areas such as Seoul Station, Myong Dong, East Gate, and north to Mia Dong and Suyuri. The orange line is almost as long and traverses the city, north and west, stopping at key places such as the Seoul Express Bus Terminal, Apkujong Dong, Ulchiro, Chongno, Changdok and Kyongbok Palaces and the Independence Gate. The red line is the shortest and basically runs through the downtown providing major transfer points to the other lines.

Designed to be very user-friendly there are plenty of signs in English and Korean to guide passengers. Large maps at every stop and smaller ones above every door on the subway, display all the lines and stops. While riding, a recorded voice calls out the stop ahead and the one following, so it's easy to keep on the right track, so to speak. After exiting, color coded signs again show the way out or to a transfer point of a connecting line. From certain spots it's even possible to transfer to a train that travels to outlying cities such as Suwon or Inchon. Some of the underground stops are uniquely designed and very attractive. The one at Chungmuro, on the orange line, is modeled like a cave and is very aesthetic. All the stops are clean and graffiti-free, and most have little shops and restaurants for commuter convenience.

The basic fare is about 45 cents (350 won) and will

purchase travel almost anywhere in the city. Tickets can be purchased over the counter or from a dispensing machine very easily. Select locations have heavy traffic during rush hours but most are not uncomfortably crowded during off periods.

The key to riding the subway is looking at a map and knowing where you want to go. The rest is easy and not only fun but an inexpensive, safe and quick way to see much of the city without the worry of traffic or parking. So ride the subway and visit Seoul's "land down under. "

TRAIN — CONVENIENT FOR LONG TRIPS

The Korea National Railroad provides four classes of train service to almost anywhere passengers might want to travel. The quickest and most comfortable are the Saemaul trains. Equipped with modern air conditioned cars, with additional leg room for added comfort, they travel frequently to key cities throughout the peninsula. This service is naturally more expensive but Saemaul has two fares, economy and first class. Always choose first class as the fare is worth the few dollar's difference. The Mugunghwa Express trains are also popular but stop more frequently than Saemaul. Mugunghwa does reach several more destinations than Saemaul however, so in some cases it may be the fastest way to travel. Descending into the lower two classes, Tongil, and Pidulgi, the service is more primitive and the stops far more frequent. This adds much time to the trip but the fare is less expensive and for foreigners who are not in a hurry it's a nice way to see the smaller country towns of Korea.

Rail travel is fast and convenient and provides a wonderful view of the scenic countryside. Tickets are sold at train stations, some tourist centers and the KNTC Tourist Information Center. Customers may purchase tickets up to three months in advance and, during peak holiday travel periods, it is wise to take advantage of advance ticket purchase.

AIRPLANE

Airlines - Two national carriers, Korean Airlines and Asiana, fly to all large domestic cities. A host of international carriers also visit Korea. The following is a list of common carriers and their telephone numbers.

Aeroflot	569 - 3271
Air France	773 - 3151
Alitalia Airlines	779 - 1677
All Nippon Airways (ANA)	752 - 5500
Asiana	774 - 4000
British Airways	774 - 5511
Cathay Pacific	773 - 0321
China Airlines	773 - 2273
Continental	773 - 0100
Delta	754 - 1921
Federal Express	754 - 5011
Garuda Indonesia Airways	773 - 2092
Japan Airlines (JAL)	757 - 1711
Japan Air System (JAS)	752 - 9090
Korean Airlines (KAL)	756 - 2000
Lauda Air	776 - 9607
Lufthansa	538 - 5141
Malaysia Airlines	777 - 7761
Nippon Cargo Airlines	775 - 3921
Northwest Airlines	734 - 7800
Philippine Airlines	774 - 3581
Quantas Airways	777 - 6871
Royal Dutch Airline (KLM)	755 - 7040
Singapore Airlines	755 - 1226
Swiss Air	757 - 8901
Thai Airways	754 - 9960
United Airlines	757 - 1691
VASP Brazilian Airlines	779 - 5651

Airports - Three international airports in Korea are located in Seoul, Pusan and Cheju Island. Kimpo International Airport, in the capital, is by far the largest. It has three terminals, one domestic and two international. International terminal #1 is the older of the two and houses all but nine of the international carriers. The bottom floor contains an arrival area and various informational booths to assist travelers as they enter Korea. The second floor functions as the departure area and contains the respective airline check-in counters. International terminal #2 houses both Korean Carriers and Swiss Air, Continental, Malaysia, Garuda, Lauda, Lufthansa, and Quantas airlines. It is newer and more modern but its layout is similar to terminal #1 in that the first and second floors are for arrivals and departures respectively. The airports at Pusan and Cheju are smaller but modern and efficient.

All persons departing the country are required to pay an airport tax of 7,200 won (a little over $9.00). There is also a domestic airport tax of 1,000 won. Passengers must pay in won so be prepared for this requirement upon departure. Passengers may pay the tax at the airport bank where, of course, they will change foreign currency into won.

City Air Terminal (KCAT) - Can Save You Time - Located in the southern business district of Samsongdong, it is conveniently situated behind the Korean Exhibition Center and the 56 story Korean Trade center. Deluxe hotels and excellent shopping are also close by. If operating in the vicinity of this area and planning travel through Kimpo airport, KCAT can help. Three major airlines, Asiana, Northwest and Cathay Pacific, have ticket counters and baggage checkin at KCAT. For international flights passengers should arrive 2 1/2 hours early. Passengers may even process immigration at the terminal. From there they may catch a nonstop limousine bus to the airport for only 2,000 won (oneway). It's about a one-hour drive to the airport and this service beats the often grinding drive, through heavy traffic, to Kimpo. Buses leave every 15 minutes and passengers ride in a comfortable, air conditioned vehicle, unburdened by traffic or parking hassles. The bus stops at all three Kimpo terminals. Consider this option when planning future departures.

8

LANGUAGE

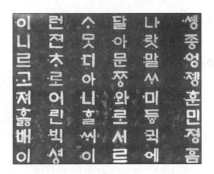

BACKGROUND

The spoken Korean language has a history as old as its people. However, the Korean written language, *Hangul*, has only been in existence for about five and a half centuries. Before *Hangul*, Koreans expressed their spoken language, in writing, using Chinese characters. Chinese and Korean are two very different languages. Chinese is written using individual ideographs or characters, each with its own meaning. There is no alphabet and thousands of these characters must be memorized to be considered literate. Much study was required to master these characters and it was very difficult for all, but the elite, to devote enough time to become literate. In the early part of the 15th century, King Sejong, one of Korea's wisest rulers, decided to develop a simple alphabet that could be quickly learned by all his subjects. He assembled a group of scholars and directed them to devise such a writing system. After years of effort they produced *Hangul* in 1443, originally, a simple 28 letter alphabet which was later reduced to 24 letters, 10 vowels and 14 consonants. King Sejong spent a few years refining it and presented it to his people in 1446. This simple phonetic alphabet could be learned quickly and eventually became popular with the masses. The intelligentsia, however, complained that *Hangul* would prevent the proper study of the Chinese classics and other classic literature. *Hangul* ultimately triumphed and because of its simplicity was soon championed by the common people.

LEARNING THE ALPHABET
— A SMALL INVESTMENT YIELDS MUCH

As previously stated, *Hangul* is a simple phonetic alphabet some foreigners have learned in as little as a few hours. There are quite a few advantages to taking time to master this wonderful system. As soon as the beginner can pronounce the letters he will instantly be able to read signs of all kinds, business cards, maps and many other messages. In addition, Koreans will appreciate and be impressed by the effort. This small investment will yield advantages hundreds of times over. Many businessmen, and visitors to Korea, have taken this basic step and have never regretted it. For anyone intending to develop a long-term business relationship with Korea, learning *Hangul* is a must, but even if a person plans to remain only a short time it can be helpful and is relatively simple to learn. The following is a chart to help you get started.

	ㅏ[a]	ㅑ[ya]	ㅓ[ŏ]	ㅕ[yo]	ㅗ[o]	ㅛ[yo]	ㅜ[u]	ㅠ[yu]	ㅡ[ŭ]	ㅣ[i]
ㄱ[k,g]	가	갸	거	겨	고	교	구	규	그	기
ㄴ[n]	나	냐	너	녀	노	뇨	누	뉴	느	니
ㄷ[t,d]	다	댜	더	뎌	도	됴	두	듀	드	디
ㄹ[r,l]	라	랴	러	려	로	료	루	류	르	리
ㅁ[m]	마	먀	머	며	모	묘	무	뮤	므	미
ㅂ[p,b]	바	뱌	버	벼	보	뵤	부	뷰	브	비
ㅅ[s,sh]	사	샤	서	셔	소	쇼	수	슈	스	시
ㅇ	아	야	어	여	오	요	우	유	으	이
ㅈ[ch,j]	자	쟈	저	져	조	죠	주	쥬	즈	지
ㅊ[ch']	차	챠	처	쳐	초	쵸	추	츄	츠	치
ㅋ[k']	카	캬	커	켜	코	쿄	쿠	큐	크	키
ㅌ[t']	타	탸	터	텨	토	툐	투	튜	트	티
ㅍ[p']	파	퍄	퍼	펴	포	표	푸	퓨	프	피
ㅎ[h]	하	햐	허	혀	호	효	후	휴	흐	히

Chart of Hangul

As can be seen from the information in the chart, there are some letters in the English alphabet that do not appear in the Korean. For example, Korean has no letter "f". This would not normally pose a problem since logically Korean has no words using the "f" sound. But modern Korean has had to accommodate the almost universal language of English and has adopted many English words into Korean. Words like family, Fanta, or "f" sounding words like telephone, are difficult for Koreans to pronounce and so the "f" is usually delivered like a "p", rendering pamily for family, and pone for phone. It's even more confusing when the mistranslation forms other closely sounding words, for example discerning the difference between competent and confident. Some "f" words, are translated using an "h", meaning Fanta (the soda pop) becomes hanta. Another letter absent in Korean is "z". This poses problems not only for pure "z" words like zebra and zoo, but "z" sounding words like cheese, dessert and desire. Koreans most commonly substitute a "j" in these instances resulting in jebra and joo.

One last note; *Hangul* is the Korean alphabet not the Korean language. Foreigners sometimes make the mistake of saying they are learning to "speak *Hangul.*" A person does not speak the alphabet (*Hangul*) but can learn to speak the Korean language (Hankuk Mal).

USE OF CHINESE CHARACTERS
— CLEARING THE CONFUSION

Even after all that has been described about the wonderful development of *Hangul* it may be surprising to learn that Chinese Characters (*Hanmun*) still appear in newspapers and government documents. Even after the introduction of *Hangul*, the ability to read and write Chinese was a means and access to power. It was a sign of education, good breeding and status. Even today it is essential to recognize at least some characters to function well. *Hanmun* is very useful in clarifying certain thoughts. As previously stated, each character expresses one thought so *Hanmun* can be used to clarify words that have double meanings. As an international industrialized country Koreans recognize the economic benefit of learning Chinese. Beginning in 1994, primary schools increased their instruction in Chinese characters and it has been reported that some large Korean corporations are testing knowledge of *Hanmun* as part of the recruitment process for new employees.

POLITENESS
— MANNERS CAN CEMENT RELATIONSHIPS

Language is culture-based so culture determines how a language is used. Oriental manners are world renowned and Korea is no exception. The Korean language reflects the importance of courtesy by design. The very structure discloses status, manners and position in the hierarchy. Several levels of politeness, or honorifics, may be chosen from when speaking depending on the status of the speaker and receiver. For example, a father talking to his son will use a rough, or blunt form while two acquaintances may choose to converse in a polite informal form. An employee talking to his boss may use a very respectful form. The difference lies in the suffix attached to the verb at the end of the sentence. Mixing or improperly using them can cause insult, embarassment or anger.

Honorifics are also incorporated directly into the vocabulary. For example, the verb *mokda* (to eat) has two other forms, *dushida*, and *chapsushida* which reflect increasing forms of politeness. Some nouns are similarly affected. For example, the simple form for house, *chip*, is followed by *daek*, and *cha taek*, which are increasingly polite.

If all this isn't confusing enough remember honorifics may be used in reference to someone else but never when referring to yourself. Also remember this, when referring to another it is not common, as in English, to use the pronoun "you". "You" as a subject is most often omitted, as it is understood. So, "Are you going to the store?" would be rendered "Going to the store?". Foreigners frequently try to translate English sentences, word for word, which usually cannot be done correctly.

As a foreigner some allowances are made. Koreans are usually delighted that a foreigner will even try to speak their language. Even the most meager attempts will be rewarded with compliments of how "perfectly" the person speaks Korean. However, to really become a hit, take the time to learn polite Korean and use the most polite form in conversation. Koreans will deeply appreciate the effort and be more inclined to establish and maintain solid friendships.

Take the time to learn a few key phrases (see chapter 9) and practice before using them in public. When trying to incorporate additional phrases always inquire as to the most polite way to express that thought. Foreigners who use the most polite form will rarely offend another and will likely be viewed as a gentleman or lady.

AVOIDING SLANG AND JAPANESE LOAN WORDS

Even though a foreigner does not take up learning the Korean language, many pick up at least a few Korean words during their stay. There is a great temptation to acquire slang words as part of the vocabulary. Some feel such words make them more familiar and closer to their Korean friends. Quite the contrary is true. As already mentioned, politeness is the key to making a good impression. Koreans may laugh at the use of slang by a foreigner but inside they are wincing. Also, try not to add Japanese loan words to your vocabulary and mistakenly use them as Korean. Words like "mamasan," "hooch", "taksan" or "skosi," are all words left over from the Japanese occupation or perpetuated by visitors of the bar town's outside most military camps. It is very embarrassing, but I have witnessed it on several occasions, when a visitor meeting Koreans at a social function proudly proclaims he has learned "skosi" Korean but he likes the country "taksan" (trying to convey he has learned a little Korean but likes the country very much). Make sure whatever words or phases are learned are ones that a person would be proud to speak in any company. It will result in much more benefit than may be readily apparent.

9

USEFUL KOREAN PHRASES

The following phrases are divided by syllable. Knowing the number of syllables can sometimes assist in rendering the proper pronunciation.

GREETINGS

How Are You?   Ahn Nyong Ha Shim Nee Kka?

This greeting is used regardless of time of day. It is also used in response to the same greeting.

Hello   Yo Bo Sae Yo

Used differently than you might expect. It is not used as a casual greeting between people meeting face to face, as we might do in the West. It is used as a greeting when answering the telephone however. It is also used to get someone's attention, for example, calling to a passer-by from your car to ask directions.

Nice To Meet You   Man Na So Pahn Gahp Sum
                     Ni Da

This may be used in meeting someone for the first time. Upon subsequent meetings after some lapse of contact you may use a shortened version (Pahn Gahp Sum Ni Da) to mean "Nice to See You."

What Is Your Name   Ee Rum Ee Mu O Shim Ni Kka

My Name Is Mr. Jones	Nay Ee Rum Un *Mr. Jones* Im Ni Da
Welcome (Please Come In)	O So O Ship She O
Goodbye	Ahn Nyong Hee Ka Say yo, Ahn Nyong Hee Kay Say yo

A slightly different version is used depending on whether you are staying or leaving. The word "Ka" in Korean means go, so if you are staying you say to the person leaving "go in peace"(Ahn Nyong Hee *Ka* Say Yo). The word "Kay" means stay, so the person leaving says to the person staying, "stay in peace"(Ahn Nyong Hee *Kay* Say Yo). It only takes a few tries to remember it well.

See You Again	Tto Man Nap Shi Da

APPRECIATION AND PARDONS

Thank You	Kam Sa Ham Ni Da
You're Welcome	Chon Man Ae Yo
I'm Sorry	Mi An Ham Ni Da
Excuse Me	Shil Lae Ham Ni Da
Sorry To Interrupt	Su Go Ha Shim Ni Da

A polite way to interrupt someone working in order to get their attention or ask a question. It is a kind of greeting for this specific situation.

Keep Up the Good Work	Su Go Ha Say Yo

A polite way to end a conversation with someone who is working. It acknowledges their good work and thanks them at the same time. There are hundreds of appropriate business situations for this expression. For example, you meet a receptionist and she provides directions to an office. Thank her and depart with Su Go Ha Say Yo. A man delivers an order. Thank him and send him on his way with Su Go Ha Say Yo.

Just a Moment Please	Jam Kkan Man Ki Da Ree Say Yo
I Ate Well	Chal Mo Ko Sum Ni Da

It is polite to say this after a good meal, similar in meaning to "the meal was great" or "I enjoyed the meal."

TRANSPORTATION AND SHOPPING

Do You Have···	···Sum Ni Kka
How Much Does It Cost?	Ol Ma Im Ni Kka
It Is Expensive	Be Sam Ni Da
I Will Take It	Ee Go Sul Sa Ge Sum Ni Da
Please Take Me To···	···Ro Kap Shi Da

Literally translated it means "let's go to" but this phrase can be used when boarding taxis to inform the driver of the desired destination. For example, Itaewon U Ro Kap Shi Da.

Where is	O Di Ee Sum Ni Kka

The "where is" portion actually appears at the end of the sentence, for example, "where is the bathroom" is spoken "*bathroom* O Di Ee Sum Ni Kka."

Please Give Me	Ju Say Yo

Again, the verb is always at the end of the sentence so "Please give me a beer" becomes "Maek Ju (beer) Ju Say Yo".

Suit	Yang Bok
Necktie	Naek Ta Ee
Shoes	Ku Du
Jacket	Jo Ko Ri

Furniture	Kagu
Brassware	Nod Goo Rut
Jewelry	Bo Sok
Necklace	Mok Ko Ri

EATING AND DRINKING

Hungry	Pay Go Pa Yo
Thirsty	Mok Ee Mal La Yo
Western Liquor	Yang Ju
Beer	Maek Ju
Wine	Po Do Ju
Coffee	Coppee
Tea	Hong Cha
Water	Mul

GOLF

| Please You Hit First | Mon Jo Chi Say Yo |
| Have a Good Round | Chal Chi Say Yo |

Literally means please hit well. Can be used to wish someone well before a round of golf or before they hit the ball. The past tense (Chal Chot Soy Yo) can be used after someone hits a nice shot. You may use it as a question by ending with an upward intonation. This could mean either did you have a nice shot or did you have a good round of golf.

| Give | Gi Voo |

Of course, this is the English word "give" but pronounced as two syllables with the second syllable carrying a long [u] sound. It means someone is close enough to the hole that the opponents will allow him to finish without putting it in. What is often called a gimmie putt in America.

It Landed In a Bunker   Bun Ko Ae Pa Jot Soy Yo
What Was Your Score   Myot Bon Chot Soy Yo

Can be used to ask what was the score for a particular hole or the entire game.

What Is Your Handicap   Han Di Ga Myot Bon Im Ni Kka

MISC.

Yes   Nay
No   A Nee Yo
It Is Good   Cho Sum Ni Da

I Like It   Cho Ah Ham Ni Da
Bathroom   Hwa Jang Shil

TITLES OF KEY POSITIONS

President   Sa Jang

This term is used for presidents of a company and not a country. A completely different term is used for the president of a country (Dae Tong Nyong).

Vice President   Bu Sa Jang
Chairman   Hwoe Jang
Director   Sang Moo Ee Sa
General Manager   *no exact equivalent*
Manager   Cha Jang
Section Manager   Kwa Jang
Assistant Manager   Dae Ri
Supervisor   Kay Jang

DIVISION

Bureau	Kuk
Department	Bu

10

GENERAL BUSINESS INFORMATION

CHAEBOL

No book about business in Korea would be complete without at least some information on Korean *chaebol*, or business conglomerates. Their enormous size earns them the title and there are only a few dozen worthy of the title, depending on the exact definition. Some are much older than others, a few rose in the 50's with the help of the government, others followed a decade or so later. This text is not intended to describe the *chaebol* or their histories in any detail but it would be a handicap for any foreigner doing business in Korea not to be aware of their existence and know some of the most famous names associated with them. The following list of the top ten *chaebols* are provided by Group and a sample of its core companies, followed by the next ten *chaebols* by name only:

1. Hyundai	Electronics Ind.
	Hyundai Motor
	Hyundai Oil
2. Samsung	Electronics
	Samsung Heavy Industries
	Samsung Aerospace Industries
	Samsung Petrochemical
3. Daewoo	Shipbuilding
	Daewoo Heavy Industries
	Daewoo Motor

4. LuckyGoldstar	Goldstar Electronics
	Lucky Petrochemical Corp.
	Honam Refinery
5. Sunkyong	Yukong Ltd.
	Hankuk Sangsa
	SKC
	Sunkyong Ltd.
6. Hanjin	Hanjin Heavy Industries
	Korean Air
	Hanjin Shipping
7. Ssangyong	Ssangyong Oil Refining
	Ssangyong Cement
	Ssangyong Motor
8. Kia	Kia Motors Corp.
	Asia Motors
	Kia Steel
9. Hanwha	Kyungin Energy
	Hanyang Chemical Corp.
10. Lotte	Lotte Chilsung Beverage
	Lotte Shopping

11. Kumho
12. Daelim
13. Doosan
14. Dong-Ah Construction
15. Hanil
16. Hyosung
17. Dong-kuk steel
18. Sammi
19. Halla
20. Hanyang

Foreign business persons undoubtedly have heard of most of these names or will within a short time in Korea.

ORGANIZATIONS THAT CAN HELP

AMCHAM

The American Chamber of Commerce was founded in 1953 as a nonprofit organization to promote trade and investment between Korea and the US. AMCHAM attempts to represent American business working in Korea, and act as a voice for the business community, communicating with the Korean government and business associations. They also work closely with the US Embassy to ensure cooperation between the US government and business. The Chamber consists of well over a thousand members and offers numerous services including seminars, luncheons featuring informative guest speakers, and a helpful Breakfast Briefing Program which provides key information to top executives, concerning business in Korea. A number of publications dealing with various aspects of living and working in Korea are sponsored by the Chamber. They are located in the Westin Chosun Hotel, and are open everyday during regular business hours. Their mailing address is:

> American Chamber of Commerce in Korea
> Room 307, Westin Chosun Hotel
> 87 Sokong-dong, Chung-gu, Seoul 100
> Tel: (02)752-3061 Fax: (02)755-6577

Korean Chamber of Commerce and Industry (KCCI)

Over 54 regional locations with over two million members are represented by the KCCI headquarters. While their main purpose is to assist Korean industry to develop and prosper they do maintain international affiliations with other Chambers and provide many services that can assist foreign businesses. KCCI maintains an extensive library of economic reference materials, many in English, which can be of great benefit. They also publish the Quarterly Review, *the Korean Business Directory and Guide to Investment in Korea,* all of which provide valuable information for businesses with interests in Korea. KCCI has bilateral protocols with over seventy countries and strives to promote mutual understanding with foreign businesses by sponsoring various functions which allow foreign business and government officials to meet with their Korean counterparts. The Chamber participates in other international organizations including the International Chamber of Commerce. KCCI also has an active program to promote foreign investment in Korea and introduce advanced technology transfer between Korean and foreign businesses. The Chamber handles huge numbers of requests from foreigners to pair them with the appropriate Korean business that can act as either buyer or seller for their products. KCCI can help put foreigners in touch with the right people in Korea to make their business desires become a reality more quickly and efficiently. Take advantage of the wide range of services they offer. They are located in an attractive building just across from the historic South Gate (Namdaemun) in downtown Seoul and their mailing address is:

The Korea Chamber of Commerce and Industry
45 Nandaemunno 4-ga, Chung-gu, Seoul 100-743
Tel:(02) 316-3114 Fax:(02) 757-9475

KABI

The Korean-American Business Institute is a private institution established in 1974, to facilitate international cooperation and understanding in the business community. KABI provides a number of services including consulting, management training, research and other assistance. Every year they also sponsor a comprehensive seminar on doing business in Korea (a fee is required). This organization can be helpful in arranging contacts and providing information or assistance concerning Korean government regulations and problems related with business-government relations. They are conveniently located in the President Hotel in downtown Seoul near the City Hall. Their mailing address is:

Korean-American Business Institute
Suite 808, Paik Nam Building
1883, 1-ga, Ulchiro, Chung-gu, Seoul
Tel: (02) 753-7750 Fax: (02) 752-6921

Korea Exhibition Center (KOEX)

KOEX is an enormous international trade show and convention center in the heart of the southern business district of Seoul. KOEX is part of a complete complex including the adjacent Korea World Trade Center (KWTC). KWTC is easily recognizable as it towers 55 stories high. The complex houses scores of businesses and KOEX supports over eighty international trade shows per year. Over 400 business display their products on the main floor of the complex and other support facilities are available including; the deluxe Intercontinental Hotel, Hyundai Department Store, and the Korea City Air Terminal all joined by a wonderful underground shopping mall packed with stores and restaurants. The facility fully supports business with other services such as secretarial and translation, telecommunication, postal and stationary support facilities. It is easy to reach by subway, bus, taxi or car and there is plenty of parking. There are many reasons you may eventually visit this facility and a variety of ways it can help you.

INFORMATION SOURCES
Newspapers

Both the Korea Times and Korea Herald are popular English Language dailies published in Korea. These papers might seem a little thinner than papers Westerners are used to, but they do carry the major news stories taken from international wire services and other local news, sports, culture and entertainment. A Monday edition is not published as the newspapers do not work on Sunday. Of course foreigners can subscribe to either paper or procure them at almost any hotel that caters to foreigners. Some major US newspapers and international papers are available at major hotels.

Magazines

There are a variety of English language business publications produced in Seoul. Depending on your type of business and specific interest there are various periodicals and trade journals to choose from. Most are available at better book stores throughout Korea. Others are available at book stores and business centers located within fine hotels. International editions of foreign magazines such as Newsweek, Time, etc., are also available.

11

COMMENTS OF SOME SUCCESSFUL KOREAN BUSINESSMEN

Some of Korea's most successful businessmen were kind enough to offer their opinions and observations about cultural differences that inhibit international business relations. Although they come from a variety of backgrounds and business experience, there appears to be a common thread to their advice.

Kim Woo-choong

As Chairman and founder of one of the most successful businesses in the world, the Daewoo Group, Kim is a living legend. He has been honored by numerous international organizations and foreign governments. His success story is one of perseverance and hard work. He is known as an individual with a talent for turning adversity into business opportunity. Kim is internationally respected and a look at his philosophy and business acumen will surely provide insight into Korea and operating successfully in an international environment.

Kim began his textile business in 1967 with four other people. His rapid success resulted in the acquisition of many failing companies which Kim rebuilt and made successful parts of the Daewoo Group. His endeavors quickly spread to construction, shipbuilding, aerospace and defense equipment, automobiles, electronics and a host of other products and services. By 1992, Daewoo group was ranked 41st on the Fortune 500 list of successful international business giants. Today, Daewoo can be found working in scores of cities around the world. The Daewoo name is closely associated with its founder, Chairman Kim and both are recognized and respected on five continents. Needless to say, Chairman Kim's international business experience and hard-earned lessons can be of value to the Westerner trying to work successfully in Korea. Chairman Kim has a few suggestions and words of advice. "First of all maintain a positive attitude" Kim Says. "It's part of my own philosophy and works just as well for Koreans as it does for foreigners." "Do not reveal or express your negative opinions about Korea to your Korean partners. Try to learn about Korean culture and customs before you develop an opinion. Be positive and your Korean partners will feel positive about dealing with you. Remember, in Korea, relationships are the key to business and foreigners who are adept at developing relationships will likely be the most successful. Secondly, strive to succeed in the long run. Foreigners who come to Korea for short-term profit may be disappointed. Korean relationships mature over a long period and it may take some time for foreigners to develop such contacts. Come to Korea with a commitment to work and stay for a long period. Thirdly, guard your name and reputation very carefully. Do not compromise it or dishonor it in anyway. People know you by it and you must live up to the expectation of your position. Maybe most important of all, impress your partner with your actions not your words. Of course you must be careful how you speak but, as I have said many times, it is your actions that will really move people. These are just a few of the many ways a foreigner can succeed in Korea. I encourage all foreign businessmen to come with an open mind and a willingness to learn about our country and culture. This type effort can be a major step to success."

Ryu Yong-cheol

As Vice Chairman and CEO of Dong-Ah Construction Company, Ryu has had over thirty years as a successful businessman in a number of foreign countries. Ryu is also the Vice Chairman of the Korea Roads Association and the Chairman of the Construction Committee of the Korean Chamber of Commerce and Industry. His experience in a number of top management positions and business organizations has formed some impressions of international business differences that he transformed into some insightful advice. Ryu began by mentioning that a person can learn a lot about a culture through the construction business. Dong-Ah has built offices, houses, businesses, powerplants, roads, dams, harbor facilities and a host of other facilities in numerous foreign countries. Buildings and interior designs often reflect a part of a culture, said Ryu, and by living, building and working in these countries he has learned much about intercultural relations. Dong-Ah Group is the 14th leading *chaebol* in Korea and Dong-Ah Construction, a very old and well established company.

Ryu has enjoyed working with foreigners in their lands and had plenty of good advice for foreigners coming to Korea. He said to remember that all business revolves around human relations. His philosophy, and that of most other Koreans, is "Friends first, business second." "In Korea, friendship comes before money or business." Koreans feel more comfortable conducting business with those they trust. Friendship and trust are inseparable and are developed through social activity. For foreigners to really make a good impression and develop close friendships they must interact with Koreans socially. To do so successfully they should take the time to learn Korean etiquette and customs. While basic courtesy is almost universal certain manners are emphasized even more in Korea. Respect for elders and a person's position should be observed more carefully by foreigners, said Ryu. Age and position merit a certain amount of respect of there own. This becomes especially important for young foreigners to remember when dealing with older Koreans.

Eventually, social interaction will include enjoying meals together. Ryu suggests foreigners try Korean food. Koreans often enjoy introducing a variety of their delicious foods to foreigners. Sampling some of the food creates good feelings among Koreans. Even if foreigners have not yet developed a taste for such food they should at least try it several times; they may soon find they like it.

In Ryu's opinion Koreans and Japanese are more persistent about business. In other words, they will keep trying from a number of different angles until a "no" becomes a "yes". He felt Americans were not as persistent and Europeans even less so. He advised them not to take "no" for an answer. Keep trying from many different angles, including developing the right social relationships, until they succeed. He also observed that Americans are sometimes a little too strict and legalistic. He advised those visiting Korea to loosen up and be a little more flexible. He strongly recommended that foreigners be less individualistic and learn to consider more group-oriented behavior while operating in Korea. Finally, he shared his philosophy on learning foreign languages. Ryu believes that to conduct business in a foreign country one should learn some of the target country's language and the language of at least two of its close neighbors. He did not recommend spending too much time learning it in detail, but enough to exchange polite greetings and express basic thoughts. This can be very advantageous especially in the Orient.

Cho Rae-seung

With over twenty five years' experience with Kia Motors, Cho has been President and CEO of Asia Motors since 1991. Asia Motors merged with Kia Motors in 1976 and makes many fine automobiles and trucks distributed worldwide. As the leader of a top commercial vehicle manufacturer in Korea, Cho has many unique thoughts on foreigners conducting business in Korea. President Cho and his general manager in charge of the China Project, Mr. Chung Kenam were very helpful in providing some interesting cultural perspectives foreign businessmen would be wise to consider. Cho suggested that foreigners should make a strong effort to respect the indigenous culture of Korea, and the long traditional legacy that has formed through nearly 5,000 years of history. It is wise to observe, learn and then express a positive attitude toward that culture. Koreans can quickly detect open or closed mindedness toward their culture and it has a strong influence on business relations. He believed that Koreans in general, are sensitive to how their culture is perceived by foreigners. Cho suggested that businessmen be much different than tourists. Tourists visit a short time, spend money and return home while businessmen must live and work in Korea for a specific business goal, and must develop close relationships if they hope to achieve their business objectives. Chung noted that foreigners often telegraph their impressions through various non-verbal cues. He recommended they practice a kind of "face management" carefully controlling facial expressions so that they might not indirectly reveal negatives like disappointment, boredom, insincerity or anger. Cho noted that simple things can often unintentionally make a negative impression. For example, during meetings, foreigners often refer to others, even top management personnel, as "that guy" or "this guy". Such phrases are considered impolite to Koreans and can cause an unnecessary irritant. Foreigners should try to harmonize with the mood of the meeting and consider the feelings and customs of others more in interpersonal relations. He used the analogy of speaking from a warm heart instead of a cold brain. Empathy and understanding are critical to good relations. Cho also recommended treating criticism like a poison, never giving it unless requested and then delivering it delicately and indirectly. The same could be said for refusals. It is much wiser to refuse carefully, indirectly, and gently with many warm explanations. He cautioned that business is made by feeling humans not unfeeling organizations. Foreigners should develop their relations with a positive mind, patience and much social contact. During social contact, remember once again, little things can make a difference. The foreigner who has taken the time to learn to eat with chopsticks, for example, or is willing to try Korean food and Korean liquor will create a warmer feeling with his Korean counterpart.

When dealing with an organization, Cho felt it is wise to analyze each particular company and its decision making process. Some companies are more autocratic and the owner makes most of the decisions. Others allow decisions to flow from mid management upward allowing top management to make a decision after the staff has reached some consensus. This is important to consider as it provides a clue to the level of management a businessman needs to influence in order to shape success.

These are just a few suggestions he offered to foreign businessmen interested in improving their business relations in Korea.

Park Sam-koo

Currently, Presidnet of Asiana Airlines, Park has over twenty-seven years as a businessman and has held numerous leadership positions in the Kumho group, Korea's eleventh largest conglomerate. His international business experience has made him both well known and respected in Korea and in many countries around the world. He was kind enough to share his wealth of knowledge and offer some advice to foreigners about the differences between Korean and Western cultures and what foreigners can do to help smooth intercultural relations. "I have said many times that the push for internationalization is critical to the future development of all countries of the world. The concepts of diversity, broad mindedness, and adaptability must be practiced by Koreans as well as Westerners. So of course, Koreans as well as Westerners, must learn about and accept foreign customs and culture when traveling abroad. This book however, is concerned with educating Westerners visiting Korea and how they can do their part to contribute to the fundamental ideals of globalization.

"Remember, Korea is a country of ancient tradition and manners and knowing and abiding by local customs will win the respect of the hosts. Foreigners should not be intimidated by Korean culture as Koreans are understanding hosts and appreciate a foreigner's attempts at learning our ways. Be curious and persistent at developing some basic cultural skills whether it be a few simple polite expressions in our language or just sampling some of the scores of tasty delicacies Korea has to offer. Specific customs and actions are well-described in the text of this book, but I believe the most important issue of the future is the change in attitude that must occur when Westerners reach Korea. When dealing between cultures, as different as Korea and the West, it is human nature to experience confusion and frustration when you begin life in Korea. My advice is, take the differences in stride, and trust that behind every possibly confusing aspect of Korean society there is a reason, probably backed by hundreds even thousands of years of tradition. This does not make it better nor worse than the way you are accustomed to, but it usually provides an exciting backdrop for another perspective to explore and consider. If you approach individual customs with this outlook you will not only enjoy yourself more but you will be exponentially more effective in relating to the Koreans with whom you will do business.

"Also consider that, as important as they are, we may sometimes focus too much on our differences. A closer look reveals, that regardless of nationality, we are in many ways very much alike. That may be what makes internationalization possible, our similarities provide a foundation for our relationships while an accommodating understanding of our differences adds the proper seasoning to make the mixture a successful recipe. Spend the time to learn of both, accentuating our sameness while accommodating our uniqueness, and any business person will more likely know the joy of success in modern international business.

"The future of international business in Korea is bright and many foreigners will continue to try their hand at establishing businesses here. Today and in the future, a good idea and a well-thought-out plan are not enough to succeed internationally. Regardless of the industry or field, to take advantage of the coming opportunities in Korea, foreigners will have to open their minds and hearts to the people they wish to share a business relationship with. When we know each other and can delight in the diversity of our cultures, we will achieve the necessary harmony that contributes to the most potent business success. That is the essence of globalization and the key to our mutual prosperity in the years ahead."

APPENDICES

- Suggested Reading List
- Index

SUGGESTED READING LIST

The following suggested reading list includes just a few of the many books which will help you learn more about Korean customs, culture, and history. Where appropriate, a brief explanation about the book has been provided.

CULTURE AND PHILOSOPHY

Boye De Mente. *Korean Etiquette and Ethics in Business*. Ill:NTC, 1989.

For foreigners doing business in Korea, it is a good guide to many local manners and customs. Many do's and don't's are provided that can likely be applied to your situation. It could be described as a fine primer that may spark an interest in learning more about the people and culture of Korea.

Choi, Min-Hong. *A Modern History of Korean Philosophy*. Seoul: Seong Moon Sa, 1978.

Will be better enjoyed by those more deeply interested in this subject. This book provides rather detailed explanations and history of Korean philosophy.

Crane, Paul S., *Korean Patterns*. Seoul: Royal Asiatic Society, 1978.

This book has become somewhat of a classic for foreigners interested in Korean culture. Although written rather long ago, it still provides a valuable overview of the more common aspects of Korean life.

Ha, Tae Hung. *Folk Customs and Family Life*. Seoul: Yonsei University Press, 1986.

Short explanations of some of the more esoteric customs and many of the traditional Korean holidays.

Hur, Sonja Vegdahl. *Culture Shock; Korea.* Portland: Graphic Arts Center Publishing Company, 1993.
One of a series of books on a variety of countries, this one provides a nice sample of customs and courtesies for the international traveler.

Lee, Jung Young. *Sokdam, Capsules of Korean Wisdom.* Seoul: Seoul Computer Press, 1983.
Lists 113 of Korea's favorite proverbs with brief explanations. Entertanining and educational.

Pares, Susan. *Crosscurrents.* Seoul: Seoul International Publishing House, 1986.
A general comparison of Korean culture to Western culture. Easy reading and a good introduction.

Looking at Each Other. Seoul: Seoul International Publishing House.
A short and amusing look at the difference between Korea and the West. The many concepts are well illustrated to facilitate understanding.

Yang, S.M., *Korean Customs and Etiquette.* Seoul: Moon Yang Gak, 1991.
Features short descriptions of some general Korean customs and courtesies.

NOVELS AND GENERAL INTEREST
Bond, Larry. *Red Phoenix.* New York: Warner Books, 1989.
A gripping scenario of how a future Korean War could develop. The description of student and political unrest is very well done. It's one of those books that is hard to put down. Bond created a true-to-life picture of the Korean environment.

Kim, Hyon Hee. *The Tears of My Soul.* New York: William Morrow and Company Inc, 1993.

The true story of the North Korean agent who helped blow up KAL flight 858, in November 87, killing over 100 people. Great insight into the determination of North Korea to continue in unpredictable terrorism.

Liston, Robert A. *The Pueblo Surrender.* New York: M. Evans and Company Inc. 1988.
A great between-the-lines look at this tragic incident. This book raises some interesting questions. Good reading.

Utts, Thomas C. *Korea Blue.* New York: Signet, 1991.
Sex and intrigue, an interesting spin on happenings within the US military in Korea in the 60's and 70's.

HISTORY

Clark, Donald N. *The Kwangju Uprising.* Boulder: Westview Press, 1988.
This historic incident is covered well in the less than 100 pages of this book. Best for those who have a real interest in the detail of the incident and its context in Korean history.

Han, Woo-Keun. *The History of Korea.* Honolulu: The University Press of Hawaii, 1980.
An easy to read general history of Korea which covers most important events in enough detail to make it a fine reference to help answer general historical questions.

Henderson, Gregory. *Korea: The Politics of the Vortex.* Cambridge: Harvard University Press, 1968.
A classic text of modern politics in Korea. This book is well researched and written but is best left to those with a sincere interest in the behind the scenes political developments in Korea through the 1960's.

Nahm, Andrew C., *Korea: Tradition and Transformation.*
New Jersey: Hollym, 1988.
Provides a helpful general overview of Korean history
with a focus from the Yi Dynasty(1392-1910) to present.
Photos and maps are plentiful and well placed. A handy
reference.

MILITARY

Goulden, Joseph C., *The Untold Story of the Korean War.*
New York: McGraw-Hil, 1982.
Great for understanding the inside story of the Korean
war in the context of the politics of the times. Good
reading and interesting for those with or without a
background in Korean War history.

Blair, Clay. *The Forgotten War.* Virginia: Times Books, 1987
Written in exacting detail, the length (976 pages), makes
it difficult to get through for all but the most dedicated
war enthusiasts.

Hoyt. Edwing P., *The Pusan Perimeter.* New York: Stein and
Day, 1984
The Korean War can be divided into a variety of battles
and episodes. The author has done so in a series of
interesting books of which this is only one. Check for
other titles of major battles if you have a particular
interest.

OTHERS

Conroy, Hilary. *The Japanese Seizure of Korea 1868-1910.*
Philadelphia: University of Pennsylvania Press, 1960.

Cook, Harold F. *Korea's 1884 Incident.* Seoul: Royal Asiatic
Society Korea Branch, 1972.

Deuchler, Martina. *Confucian Gentleman and Barbarian*

Envoys; The Opening of Korea 1875-1885. Seattle: University of Washington Press, 1977.

Ku, Dae-Yeol. *Korea Under Colonialism.* Seoul: Royal Asiatic Society Korea Branch, 1985.

Nelson, Frederick M. *Korea and the Old Orders in Eastern Asia.* Baton Rouge: Louisians State University Press, 1946.

Rutt, Richard. *History of the Korean People.* Seoul: Royal Asiatic Society Korea Branch, 1972.

Swartout, Robert R. *Mandarins. Gunboats and Power Politics: Owen Nickerson Denny and the International Rivalries in Korea.* University Press of Hawaii, 1980.

INDEX